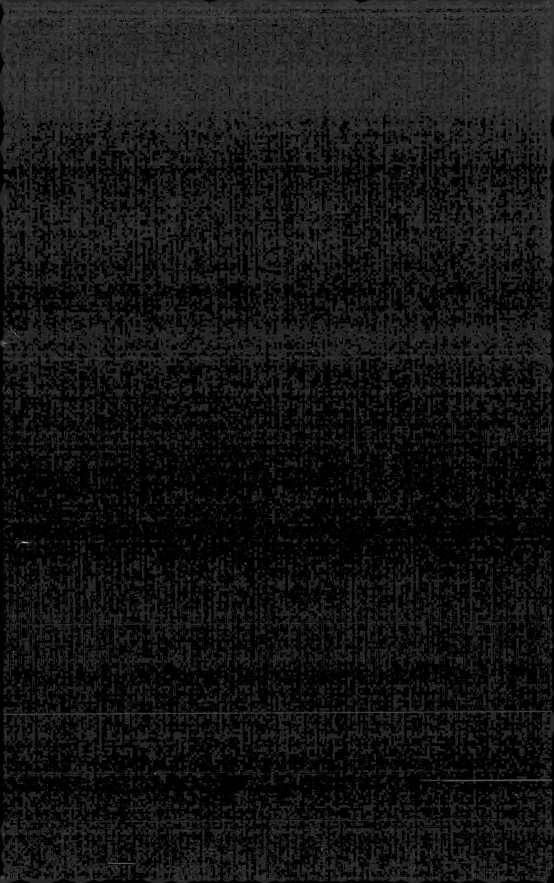

The
ADVENTURE
CAPITALISTS

The ADVENTURE CAPITALISTS

THE SUCCESS SECRETS
of Twelve High-achieving Entrepreneurs

Jeff Grout and Lynne Curry

KOGAN PAGE

YOURS TO HAVE AND TO HOLD

BUT NOT TO COPY

First published in 1998

Kogan Page Limited
120 Pentonville Road
London N1 9JN
England

Kogan Page Limited
163 Central Avenue, Suite 4
Dover, NH 03820
USA

British Library Cataloguing in Publication Data
A CIP record for this book is available from the British Library.
ISBN 0 7494 2638 1

Typeset by Deltatype Limited, Birkenhead, Merseyside
Printed and bound in Great Britain by
Biddles Ltd, Guildford and King's Lynn.

41890224

Contents

Preface

Robert Half International, the world's leading specialist recruitment consultancy, has for many years been advising its clients on both sides of the employment equation on how to aim for success. The guidance ranges from interviewing effectively to being interviewed effectively; from structuring a career to choosing a financial director; from choosing the right employer to being chosen by the right employer.

In 1994, the company brought together a group of people who knew, firsthand, and spectacularly, about being successful. The Body Shop founder Anita Roddick, Habitat creator and restaurateur Sir Terence Conran and TV executive Greg Dyke – 'father' of Roland Rat, and hugely skilful manager of TV stations – were invited to share the secrets of their achievements, and evaluate the costs and drawbacks. To the surprise and pleasure of Robert Half's UK managing director, Jeff Grout, all three happily agreed.

The result was the first three in a series of interviews before an audience of Robert Half clients, who packed the Bafta Centre in Piccadilly to be treated to amusing, frank and informative insights into the mechanics of success. The format worked so well that the first series expanded into a programme of interviews with a wide range of people successful in other fields, from entrepreneur Peter de Savary to Liverpool FC chief executive Rick Parry. Apart from their wealth and celebrity, it was noted that another common denominator was that many of them had begun life as accountants.

Grout was told he should turn their anecdotes, experiences, sagacity and acumen into a book. And here it is. We have called it *The Adventure Capitalists* (with a small apology to Ms Roddick), to reflect the verve and enthusiasm of their efforts, and hope that their willingly shared escapades and advice will instruct, interest and – yes – even inspire others.

The Subjects

Sir Terence Conran has blended design, cuisine and retail with unique success. In the 1960s he kick-started a revolution in the way the British live, with his ground-breaking modernist furniture store, Habitat. He went on to pave the way for 'own brand' retailing, before moving – via corporate retailing – to a stable of successful London restaurants and food businesses. These included the spectacular Bibendum, in the art deco building which had been the London headquarters of Michelin. Several of Conran's projects have been conceived with a view to regenerating run-down areas.

Conran sees design, aesthetics, gastronomy, retail – and gardening, another passion – as a harmonious blend of complementary interests, which is why he has the furniture-making business in the grounds of his Wiltshire home, and why he also lives 'above the shop' near his food emporia in Butlers Wharf, on the south bank of the Thames in London. And, although he is now beyond conventional retirement age, he has no intention of abandoning them, since they are not only his work but his consuming interests.

Trained as a textile designer, Conran became a furniture maker, setting up Habitat in 1964 to sell his own wares. His retail career moved into the corporate world with Storehouse, the group which encompassed Habitat, Mothercare, British Home Stores (BhS), Richard Shops and Heal & Son. He retired from Storehouse in 1990, buying back The Conran Shop on Fulham Road and redirecting his attentions towards food and design. In addition to Bibendum, his eating houses include Blueprint Café above the Design Museum, Mezzo, Le Pont de la Tour, Cantina del Ponte, the Bluebird Foodmarket and Restaurant in the King's Road, and Quaglino's in St James's. There are plans for an elegant, urban Italian restaurant in Savile Row (Sartoria) and Coq d'Argent, a rooftop-garden restaurant at No 1 Poultry, in the City of London. Conran Restaurants are also in Paris and Manhattan, and he has also opened branches of The Conran Shop in Paris, Hamburg, Tokyo, Fukuoka, London, and Melbourne.

Conran has established an eponymous style, still very much admired. His designs in essential British contemporary style for the 1997 Anglo-French summit excited great interest. He is a creative consultant to the Millennium Dome, and his design consultancy, CD Partnership, works on his own projects and on others: among them the redevelopment of the Great Eastern Hotel in the City of London and the planned Ocean Terminal at Leith, Edinburgh.

Ron Dennis is head of McLaren International, and successor to founder Bruce McLaren at the helm of the McLaren Formula One racing team. Since joining the Brabham Racing Team as a mechanic in the 1960s, he has shown a cool-headed determination to succeed as an engineer and businessman. McLaren, whose drivers have included Niki Lauda, James Hunt, Alain Prost and Ayrton Senna, has won the Constructors' Championship six times and the Drivers' Championship seven times.

McLaren, based in Ron Dennis's home town of Woking, Surrey, has also built up an enviable reputation as a company of motor engineering excellence and innovation with a turnover of more than £80m. The company offers the world's rich the opportunity to buy the revolutionary F1 road car – with a top speed of 230mph – at a cost of more than £500,000. Ron Dennis enjoys a reputation as a superlative manager – some would say the best in the country – and is a prime example of the powerful effect of ambition, determination, strategy and application.

Peter de Savary attracts epithets as freely as he breathes: mesmeric, charismatic, mind like a computer, thrives on animal instinct, charming... He has also been called a buccaneer, a tycoon, an adventurer and 'arguably Britain's purest entrepreneur'. He discovered his pronounced entrepreneurial flair as a young man in Canada. From child-minding, gardening, and teaching English, he has gone on to buy, sell and lose castles, great houses, casinos, shipyards, gentlemen's clubs, hotels and acres of industrial wasteland, making and losing millions on the way. His personal fortune of some £100 million virtually dissolved when his business empire was hit by recession in 1994. Today, his fortunes rebuilt, de Savary continues to play on the international business stage.

Married with five daughters, he says he would not be alarmed by ending his career in a two-bedroom cottage – but meanwhile, lives at Skibo Castle, north of Inverness, which he has restored to its original glory and where he has established The Carnegie Club, 'a hotel for high achievers'. He still runs other successful commercial ventures, among them an international oil business, maritime and shipyard activities. He once owned Land's End and John O'Groats at the same time, rendering the British Isles 'a Peter de Savary sandwich'. He was made Tourism Personality of the Year in 1986 by the English Tourist Board. He has sailed in the Americas Cup and the Admiral's Cup, and is chairman of the board of trustees of the Victory Trust, established to help underprivileged and/or handicapped children.

Greg Dyke, now head of the television division of media group Pearson (owners of the _Financial Times_) made his name during four years as chief executive of London Weekend Television, where he had started as a researcher. He turned LWT from a £70 million company to a £750 million company. Before that, he was credited with the birth of the legendary Roland Rat, during a year as editor-in-chief at TV-am. Returning to LWT as director of programmes, he became managing director three years later and chief executive a year after that. He left – rich but disenchanted – after Granada instituted a successful takeover.

Dyke's lack of airs, and wealth of insouciant candour, have made him a popular figure, especially with the media. But he has also become a respected figure in the industry, having sat on the ITN board and chaired the ITV council. He spoke out vigorously against the independent companies' franchising system and has remained an outspoken commentator on his own industry.

Barry Hearn is regarded as Britain's leading sports promoter, the current or past mentor of Steve Davis and Chris Eubank, Herbie Hide, Carl Crook, Francis Ampofo, Steve Collins, Jim Mcdonnell, Eamonn Loughran and Garry Delaney. An ambitious chartered accountant from a working-class background, he collided happily with snooker when he was the financial director of Kensal Investments. Although principally a fashion house, he persuaded Kensal to buy the Lucania snooker chain as an investment. TV was discovering snooker at the same time, and Hearn collaborated in turning it into a major TV sport.

Hearn is now head of the Matchroom organization, which first went into boxing – at some cost, until he learnt the business – in 1987. He plunged in at the deep end by staging the fight between Joe Bugner and Frank Bruno at Tottenham's White Hart Lane stadium, in front of 30,000 people. Hearn's informal business style belies a highly focused commercial instinct, an essential quality in the aggressive world of sports management. But his outstanding quality is his ability to spot young talent. His best break was when Steve Davis walked in to play in one of the amateur tournaments he promoted.

The name of **Prue Leith** is synonymous with good food. A South African educated in Paris, she abandoned plans to be an interpreter and became a Cordon Bleu cook in London instead. She established her own catering business from her bedsit in Earls Court before going on to set up Leith's Good Food Ltd, Leith's Restaurant and Leith's School of Food and Wine. By 1993, Leith's Good Food had 300 staff and a turnover of £13 million, and was serving some 7,000 meals a day for venues such as the Queen Elizabeth Conference Centre, the Natural History Museum, Orient Express trains and Chartered Accountants Hall.

Prue Leith has been on the board of many companies, including five years at the former British Rail, with a brief to redesign the catering. She has also been involved with the Argyll Group, the parent company of Safeway, a board member of the Halifax Building Society and of Whitbread, and chair of the Royal Society of Arts. She has written for national newspapers and been featured in documentaries, as well as writing numerous cookery books. She was trade journalist of the year in 1983, awarded the Order of the British Empire in 1989, and in 1990 was named Businesswoman of the Year.

David Lloyd comes from a tennis-playing family (his parents ate and slept tennis and his brother is John Lloyd) and became a professional tennis player as a teenager. He spent 17 years on the professional circuit, mostly as a doubles specialist; he played at Wimbledon, and was ranked in the world top 30, beating Nastase, Connor, Kodes and Gottfried. But he achieved even greater success through combining his knowledge of the game with commercial acumen. After retiring from the game, he spent half his year running indoor tennis centres in Canada, then in 1981 gambled his house and lifelong savings on the first British indoor tennis and fitness centre, in Heston, Middlesex. It took off from the first day, and Lloyd went on to build similar centres all over the country.

He later floated the business (with an issue eight times oversubscribed), enjoyed great adulation from the press, became extremely rich and proved to business writers that sport and business could mix. He was Entrepreneur of the Year in the 1994 PLC awards and his company was capitalized in 1995 at £120 million. He later sold the clubs to Whitbread, staying on as a consultant for a brief period. In 1997, he was chosen as captain of the British Davis Cup team.

Rick Parry is a chartered accountant who became chief executive of the club he had supported from childhood – Liverpool FC. He was for six years chief executive of the Premier League, responsible for negotiating a series of record-breaking media and sponsorship deals. He oversaw the competition which brought major investments in new stadia, drove up attendance figures and brought innumerable international stars to this country. He also oversaw the audit into the 'bung' scandal and transfer irregularities.

Parry, who comes from Ellesmere Port and went to Liverpool University, once had trials with Liverpool and Everton (1972–3) as goalkeeper. He failed to make the team but is still fulfilling the dreams of many fans by running the club he supports. He also helped to prepare Manchester's bid for the 1996 Olympic Games. Liked and respected inside the game, Parry is known for his dogged determination and patience. He has become a brilliant conciliator and deal-maker, gleaning experience from helping to prepare Manchester's bid for the 1996 Olympic Games.

Anita Roddick is the founder (1976) of The Body Shop, the mould-breaking chain of ethically researched and produced cosmetics shops. A fiery Italian who learnt the work ethic in her mother's cafe in West Sussex, she remains outspoken and unconventional – and one of the best-known female entrepreneurs in Britain. She still travels the world finding goods and ingredients, and meeting the people who supply them. Underlying the retail operation is Roddick's belief in the power of business to be a radical force for good. The Body Shop rejected – and continues to reject – the 'image deceit, hype and packaging excesses' of the conventional cosmetics industry.

Roddick's staff work in an informal headquarters in her home town of Littlehampton, West Sussex, where their children have a creche and where they are encouraged to express their views on first-name terms, not least via messages in the cloakrooms. She has been married for more than 25 years to Gordon Roddick, and they jointly chair Body Shop International, which operates in 45 countries. Both were instrumental in setting up *The Big Issue*, the magazine published as part of a rehabilitation project for homeless people. Meanwhile, Roddick's lack of orthodoxy has not denied her accolades from more establishment quarters, including Veuve Clicquot Businesswoman of the Year (1985), the Order of the British Empire (1976) and CBI Company of the Year in 1987.

Jack Rowell is one of the most successful rugby union managers of his generation. An Oxbridge-educated Geordie who began his career managing Gosforth, he moved to the South West through his equally successful career in business, and took over as manager of Bath RUFC. Bath's meteoric rise to triumph – eight cup victories between 1976 and 1992 and five League titles in seven years – is never likely to be surpassed.

Rowell's recognition came in the form of the offer to coach and manage England, a post he held from 1994 to 1997. In those three years England achieved two Five Nations championships (one a Grand Slam) and then a successive Triple Crown, whilst progressing to the semi-final of the Rugby World Cup in 1996.

But Rowell is more remarkable for the fact that while meeting these challenges, he was also rising to the top with Dalgety Foods. He became one of its chief executives, and conducted a high-achieving business career, at the same time as he managed first Bath, then England. He remains one of the most enigmatic figures in modern sport, renowned for his extraordinary ability to motivate.

Lord Sheppard of Didgemere was born Allen Sheppard in East London. An outstanding business career began with a degree in business administration at the London School of Economics, progressed through accountancy qualifications and culminated, after approaching 20 years in the motor industry, with more than 20 years with Grand Metropolitan. Between 1986 and 1996, as chairman and chief executive, he was constantly in the news whilst refocusing GrandMet from a 'blurred portfolio' of 28 businesses to a world-leading internationally branded food and drink business.

Knighted in 1990 and again in 1997 (KCVO) and given a seat in the House of Lords in 1994, Lord Sheppard has been one of the pre-eminent post-war business leaders. Acclaimed as a marketing and management genius, he is also known for a management style which he describes as 'a loose grip around the throat'. He has a reputation for personal warmth and humour, and a disinclination to acquire airs, despite being honoured with a string of professional and personal accolades.

Chris Wright is chairman of Chrysalis Group plc, a publicly quoted media, music and entertainment company, and chairman of Loftus Road plc, owner of both Queen Park Rangers Football Club and Wasps Rugby Club. Born in a farming family in Lincolnshire, he spent his student years (politics and modern history at Manchester) as entertainments' manager of the student council. At the age of 22 he and his then partner, Terry Ellis, started the Ellis Wright agency, renamed Chrysalis a year later. It became one of the most successful independent record and music companies in the world, with artists such as Procol Harum, Jethro Tull, Ten Years After, Debbie Harry, Billy Idol, Pat Benatar, Spandau Ballet, Huey Lewis and the News and Sinead O'Connor.

Chrysalis later sold its original record label to Thorn EMI, but retained extensive music publishing interests, and started a new record company under the name of Echo in 1993. This is now one of the largest independent music publishing companies in the world. Chrysalis – also involved in TV production, sports programming, recording studios and background music systems – is the second largest independent television production company both in the UK and the Netherlands, owning such stations as Heart 106.2FM in London, Heart 100.7FM in the Midlands and Galaxy dance stations in the West Country, South Wales, Yorkshire and Greater Manchester.

More recently, Wright – a keen sports fan and tennis player – set up Loftus Road plc to buy his beloved Queens Park Rangers, as well as the Wasps Rugby Club. His company also has a basketball team, the Sheffield Sharks, while Wright himself owns racehorses at his stud farm in the Cotswolds.

The Authors

Jeff Grout is the UK managing director of Robert Half International, the largest specialist recruitment consultancy in the world. A graduate of the London School of Economics, he joined Robert Half as a recruiter at the age of 28, after an eclectic career as a van driver, passport office administrator, cleaner, world traveller, chartered town planner and, penultimately, a labourer in Edgware, north London. The building site was next door to the library where he found the newspaper containing the advertisement for his first job with Robert Half.

Since then (to the relief of his family) he has remained with Robert Half and built up the UK operation from two offices and 12 staff into a business with a domestic turnover of £50 million, 17 offices and nearly 300 staff. At the tender age of 46, he is one of the longest-serving MDs in his field.

His accumulated expertise in all aspects of recruitment mean that he is often in demand as a commentator and columnist. He has collaborated with the BBC in producing an interview training video and has run interview technique courses for a number of leading companies, including Marks & Spencer, Lloyds Bank, British Airways, Merrill Lynch, Guinness and Lever Brothers.

Lynne Curry is a freelance writer who cut her teeth on newspapers at the seaside and in the provinces, where she won a couple of awards before moving to London and moving out again at speed. She now lives on the coast in Somerset and works for a variety of newspapers, magazines and organizations in London and the South West.

1 GENESIS
In the beginning was the idea

As a creative retailer, my belief is simply that if reasonable and intelligent people are offered products that are well made, well designed, work well, are of a decent quality and at a price they can afford, then they will like and buy them.

Sir Terence Conran, designer, retailer and restaurateur.

If everyone found their way to fame and fortune by signing up undiscovered rock groups – *pace,* Chris Wright – the suburban avenues of Britain would be crowded with talent-spotters listening for the clash of discordant acoustic guitars from pulsating adolescent bedrooms.

Which is another way of saying that, at some stage of the elusive, unpredictable, unscientific business of becoming successful, there is always a grain of originality.

It may be an idea in the true spirit of entrepreneurism: spotting that gap in the market to which most of us have been blind. Or it may be a winning combination of factors: luck, timing, hard graft and charm; perception, wit, brains and the right connections; academic failure, willingness to seize a chance, memories of a tin-bath working-class background and being in the right hotel lift at the right time. Readers who doubt the influence of happy coincidence should read on. The combinations of nature and nurture that contribute to success are endless.

It may no longer be a realistic proposition to sit at a kitchen table mixing the potion that captures the spirit of the age – would CKOne have been the olfactory sensation of the early Nineties if it had come from a test tube in Teesside rather than from the amply resourced stable of Calvin Klein? – but the day that people cease to rise to the top of their field will be the end of civilization as we know it. Although it would be dishonest to suggest that The Body Shop founder Anita Roddick's path could be retrodden with the same results, history never fails to offer us lessons. We can learn from those who have gone before us.

However, there is one common factor linking all our Adventure Capitalists: not one is the product of an institution established to help them to get where they are. Few owe their success to public schools, or even to business schools. Even those who were lucky enough to go – and Greg Dyke went to Harvard – viewed the process as one of consolidation rather than inspiration.

So how did they start? What can we glean from their early faltering steps? Did they spot that magical gap in the market, or did they merely slog? Well, whatever the other factors, the Calvinist ethic is corroborated.

> A capacity for hard work, whether in the entrepreneurial or the managerial, whether the goal be conventional or venturesome, is essential from the outset. A degree of industriousness characterizes each beginning. Some set themselves a goal and worked assiduously towards it. Others were less certain of the end they had in mind, but slogged all the same.

Barry Hearn, whose mother was cleaning houses for the better-offs of Buckhurst Hill when he was a child, was aiming for a qualification in accountancy from the day he passed his 11-plus examination.

'My mother told me to aim for accountancy when I was 11 – she was cleaning houses for a chap who owned a lot of local newspapers and he told her in passing, "Tell your son to be a chartered accountant; I've never seen a poor one." And it stuck. I was telling my careers masters at grammar school that I was going to be a chartered accountant before I had any idea of what a chartered accountant did.'

Hearn qualified with Bristow Burrell, then went to Thomson McClintock. 'They were still a fairly old Scottish company and I was going through one of my flash periods – which has lasted about 47 years. I had this great phrase that making money is fabulous, but there is nothing like getting even. I would arrive at

Thomson McClintock in a white suit, and it was probably horrendous, but in those days I used to think I was the business.'

Even at the tender age of 21 – and he was one of the youngest people ever to qualify as a chartered accountant – Hearn was showing signs of the personal qualities that would propel him beyond his peers. He was ambitious. His working-class background had given him somewhere to go and something to prove, and he was single-minded. He was dedicating his energies to his goal. By the standards of his later attainment, this was modest – a one-man accountancy practice in Sawbridgeworth – but he was moving towards it.

Working days at Thomson McClintock (where he still recalls meeting a senior partner in the lift in his white suit, and being peered at in a manner only possible with a pair of half-moon spectacles), he worked nights in his own private practice. Unconventionally for a chartered accountant, he also had a car-washing round. His method of recruiting new clients for his unofficial practice – as opposed to the car washing – was to solicit those who thought TM's fees were too high. 'Anyone at Thomson who didn't like the fees, I used to just nick them. It was quite straightforward really.'

Hearn recalls the attitude that went with the suit:

> I was an aggressive son-of-a-bitch in those days. I had about 80 clients and this wonderful feeling you have when you're first married and the world is your oyster. I'd meet my wife at the station and she'd cook the dinner and then I'd go upstairs to one bedroom to work and then we'd cross half-way through the night as she got the typing for the next day. It was great to maintain 80 clients in those days, and I think I earned gross fees of about £5,000 a year, which was a lot of money in 1970, and certainly more than I was earning at Thomas McClintock. I think I was on about £3,500, which I thought was a fortune, a fortune! It supplemented the lifestyle that I wanted to lead.

Prue Leith was inspired to become a cook by watching her French 'landlady' when she was in Paris studying to become an interpreter, after an education that included Cape Town University and the Sorbonne. She was not frightened of graft or of doing whatever it took to get started. Her bedsit was her only resource, but she decided she could put a foot in the door of commercial catering by using its assets (dressing table, any other flat surface) to accommodate the sandwiches she might prepare for directors' lunches. When her home-based catering service expanded to more elaborate spreads, the bath came into its own – for lobster.

> I didn't have any money, but every cook who desires to have a business really wants a restaurant. They may kid themselves that they don't, but it's like usherettes – every usherette wants to be a movie star, and every cook wants a restaurant. But I didn't have any money, so I thought I'd better become a caterer and go and cook people's meals. I had this bed-sit in Earls Court, which was brilliant because the landlady didn't have any sense of smell. She never knew that upstairs I was preparing these great meals – lobsters in the bath and sandwiches all over the dressing table. It wasn't very hygienic.

For Jack Rowell, the first taste of graft – long before the rugby coaching began – was his accountancy examinations. He knew from the age of 16 that he wanted a career in business, and the area he preferred was finance. His school careers guidance counsellor told him that chartered accountancy was the best possible business base from which to pursue a business career. To pave the way, he studied economics at university, and went on to secure articles with a firm in Middlesbrough. The experience is etched on his memory: 'Three years' articles, average pay £6 a week, supply your own quill pen and ink. It was hard work.' Rowell qualified, but his individualistic, non-conformist temperament was already chafing against the conventions and hierarchies that surrounded him: 'Nothing wrong with the accountancy profession in any way at all – in fact, it's a first-class base for a career. But I wasn't cut out for the profession, as I found out.'

Lord Sheppard, who became known for his business management and marketing skills, followed the industry path.

> My father was an engine driver and my mother a part-time bank clerk and none of us had been in management, so we didn't actually know anything about it. I remember my father saying to me – I must have been around 12 – did I know what an accountant was. I said no, but was it something to do with numbers? My father said somebody at work had a friend whose brother-in-law was an accountant and made a lot of money. 'You're good at numbers, so why don't you become an accountant?' he said.

Sheppard went on to take a degree in economics, industry and trade at the London School of Economics. National Service followed and, with his nose still to the grindstone, he used that time to take examinations in cost and management accounting and to gain a qualification as a chartered company secretary. He also lectured part time at Nottingham Technical College. It could have been a career change, but he hated what he saw as the excessive bureaucracy of the Army. On his release, he joined the Ford Motor Company as a junior financial analyst. He was never an accountant in the pure sense – 'I got no fun from balancing balance sheets' – and from the beginning, enjoyed a more active role that hinted at his future. 'As a junior financial analyst at Ford the job, in part, was to go out, in the late Fifties and early Sixties, and to be able to outswear the Manchester group who were running manufacturing and to get them to improve what they were doing.'

Ron Dennis, Formula One supremo, was focused from the beginning. He studied vehicle technology at Guildford Technical College, not far from his home in Woking, Surrey. After finishing he was apprenticed to the Cooper Racing Company as a mechanic. He was young, and he was bold. Within two years he had been appointed chief mechanic to Sir Jack Brabham's racing team. With the confidence of youth, he put a proposition to the organization.

I said, 'You give me two of your cars and I'll run them in the European Formula Two Championship. At the end of the year I'll give them back to you and pay the difference between their new price and what they're worth second-hand.' This was in 1971, the first year that I went motor racing as a team owner, in partnership with another young guy at the time. We hire-purchased the engines – and these were racing engines – as well as the truck in which we transported the cars. We did everything ourselves; we maintained the cars, managed the cars, even though they didn't belong to us.

If you think about it in retrospect, you might well conclude that we were lunatics. Yet the fact is that the standards of the Formula Two category at that time were so low compared with Formula One, and we were all from F1 backgrounds. I had been chief mechanic and sometime team manager on the Brabham Grand Prix team. I knew that if I tackled this challenge as a team owner, we could raise the standards of that category to fresh levels, which is what we did.

The experience he gained establishing and operating this team – called Rondel Racing – marked the beginning of Dennis's path to McLaren. From knowing what he wanted to do, Dennis pursued the goal mechanically and with application, fired on by a large dose of spirit.

Greg Dyke, who built up London Weekend Television into a hugely successful company, grafted at the coalface in his early days in TV. After four or five years as a researcher, he devised the *Six O'Clock Show*, which starred Michael Aspel, Janet Street-Porter and Danny Baker. It wasn't dirty or dangerous, but it was tough, and it reduced less stalwart individuals to tears, as Dyke recalls:

> Anyone who tells you that popular programming is easy – forget it. It's much tougher. Making programmes that are applauded by your peers is much easier than making programmes where the criterion is did they or didn't they laugh. If you've got a studio audience, it's instant. I've seen people work all week to make them laugh and they didn't, then go home in tears.

He was not put off.

Rick Parry is the chief executive of Liverpool Football Club and the organizational, tactical and administrative power who established the Premier League of English football clubs. He is known as a strategist *par excellence*. But the starting point of his career, which led to him running the football club he has supported since his youth, had only one essential element. The rest was application. 'I had no career plan,' Parry says. 'I've never had a career plan other than having some vague aspiration to work in sport.' The aspiration survived an early setback, when he had trials for Liverpool and Everton at the age of 17, as a goalie, but was not taken on – 'I'll always believe I should have made it, but there we are.'

Parry's father persuaded him to get a qualification.

> My father was a PE lecturer and I always wanted to work in sport. I wanted to be a footballer, clearly, and I thought being a PE teacher would be not a bad next-best option. He dissuaded me from that on the basis that he saw far too many 40-year-old arthritic PE teachers fed up with running around muddy playing fields and suggested that I should get a professional qualification before working in sport. He suggested sports medicine, but I didn't like the sight of blood so I

couldn't become a doctor, and I guess I sort of stumbled into accountancy on the basis that I didn't have the faintest idea what I really
wanted to do when I left university.

Parry enjoyed his accountancy training and still uses it on a daily
basis, citing its basic disciplines as an asset. Discipline and
method have been his by-words in new ventures, as when he
began the task that was to raise his public profile – putting
together the Premier League. It was his capacity for objective
analysis that attracted the attention of Graham Kelly, then chief
executive of the Football League. Parry was sent to the League as
a consultant by Ernst & Young, his employers in the late 1980s.
Gaining consensus among 20 football chairmen was difficult, as
he recalls:

I was working as a consultant initially to the FA, and the FA called all
the first division clubs to a meeting in April 1991 to unveil the plans. We
had the outline of what the Premier League would look like, and some
projections on the money. The idea was the League was going to be run
very much by and within the FA. True to form one of the chairmen,
who'll remain nameless, said, 'We might not want to be within the FA,
we might want our own League. We should meet on our own to decide
what we want to do.' One of the other chairmen said, 'Well, that's a stupid idea because every time we have a meeting it's complete chaos, and
we ought to have someone to chair it.' Somebody else said, 'Well, that's
hopeless, because every time one of us chairs it we all fall out again
because nobody trusts him. We need an independent chairman.'

I should have ducked at that point, because it was clear I was the only
person in the room with a vestige of independence. So somebody said,
'You'd better chair the first meeting.' The prospect filled me with horror,
knowing some of the characters around the room. This is where basic
consultancy disciplines come in. I said I'd chair the meeting, but not for
a month, and before I did it I wanted to spend half a day with each of
them and find out what each of their aspirations were. I went round
and saw each of them in a fairly structured way, with a carefully drawn-
out set of questions. The risk was they'd be poles apart, with the big
clubs wanting the breakaway, the smaller clubs not. We sifted all the
information and analysed all the information – quite a task in itself –
trying to come up with areas of common interest so that when we had
the meeting we could say, 'Right, fellows, here are the 12 areas you all
agreed on. Is that fair?'

Few have turned honest slog to better advantage than Anita Roddick. Hard work played a major role in her working life. She gave up her job as a teacher when she and her husband, Gordon, were expecting their first child.

> I found when I was pregnant there was no way I could do a good job teaching. So we looked at how we could earn money. We found a little house and converted it into something like Fawlty Towers. We then owned a restaurant, which was like a fern restaurant in San Francisco in the Sixties or Seventies; lots of empty spaces and lots of ferns. It was fantastic. It's a great recipe – a great dress rehearsal for running a business, because you're working in other people's leisure time. It nearly killed us. It worked, and it was a wonderful avenue of activism. We had every activist group there, but it was slowly killing us, and Gordon said, 'Let's pack it up.' I wanted something controllable, small, like you lock up and unlock, and to see the kids, because we had two babies.

She came up with the idea of the The Body Shop to sell the natural products she had seen used on her travels. He was less enthusiastic, initially labelling it 'sissyish', but she persisted, and at the time when her husband was going off to America to ride a horse from Buenos Aires to New York – a long-held ambition which she supported – she had set up a little shop in a back street in Brighton, near her home town, with the goal of taking £100 a week. 'If I didn't, I would put the products in the big old log basket to knock on doors to sell the products. That's survival. That's the stuff of real entrepreneurship.'

So great ideas and great careers can owe their beginnings to hard work and a fairly conventional approach – but this is usually just part of the recipe. What about the maverick streak which entrepreneurs, especially, are supposed to tote around in their personal armoury? It exists, for sure, and in some of our Adventure Capitalists is a vein clearly visible from the beginning. Mavericks are daring – always – often willing to get their hands dirty, and often congenitally or culturally equipped with a buoyancy denied to less extrovert characters.

Here is the maverick and entrepreneur _par excellence_, Peter de Savary, on the birth of what became a multicoloured and multicultural business empire, ranging from a casino – sold after his mother refused to speak to him during his period of ownership – to a shipyard. The story begins straight from Charterhouse public school. In fact, slightly earlier than planned, as he had formed a short-lived attachment to his housemaster's _au pair_, and his father was asked, politely, to reconsider his son's future educational options. At a loose end, he joined his mother and stepfather in Canada, where he started by mowing lawns.

> It's the first time I realized I was an entrepreneur. I bought an old Pontiac car for $50. I had a lawn mower and some garden tools and got some jobs with people, doing their gardens. I noticed most of them had children, and I thought how much else could I do for them, so I offered to baby-sit. Then I realized I had an English education and an English accent, and I realized some of these children perhaps would benefit from tuition. So I offered my services as an English tutor, covering all subjects. I had a number of clients who paid me to do the garden, paid me to do the baby-sitting, paid me to teach their children. This was the first taste of how you could package something and make two and two come to five.

Sometimes de Savary could not answer the children's questions. He got round this by telling the children to go away and think about possible solutions to their questions, while he asked his girlfriend, Anne. Meanwhile, the parents were marvelling at his technique of making their children think. De Savary was in love with the business of being an entrepreneur long before he sorted out the ideas that would establish his name as the essence of that phenomenon.

> The whole thing about being an entrepreneur is that feeling, and that great surge of enthusiasm, when you realize that unlike the accountant, two and two isn't coming to four, but five or six; there's more in the package. There's a feeling of added value, and you've created something. I believe you have to be creative. I am not a speculator in the market. The only shares I've ever bought have always gone down. The only market risks I've ever taken, thinking the trend would go the other way, have always gone wrong. I've always tried to be in the busi-

ness of creating something, building something, starting new businesses, finding wasting assets, underused assets. I have never disassembled a business, always augmented and added to them. It is sheer excitement. I can remember today, all those years ago when I suddenly twigged that Mr and Mrs Wally Booth, the senior vice-president of the Ford Motor Company and his wife, were giving me three pay cheques in the same week.

In the *Sunday Telegraph* in 1985, de Savary described his career as 'a slow burn. As you meet more people and gain experience, your transactions tend to become bigger... I work bloody hard, concentrate, find the reality of the situation, cut the cloth, get some aggression.'

Many years and many ups and downs later, de Savary added Skibo Castle, in the Scottish Highlands, to his property portfolio . It was not a purchase made with the benefit of fair economic winds, but de Savary was not to be put off when his 'weekend cottage', built by the engineer Andrew Carnegie, looked set to turn into a longer-term turkey as the recession of the early Nineties took hold.

> I realized I would never in my life again – perhaps as I was approaching 50 – just have the sheer balls to buy something like that. It is quite daunting to actually buy something like that. I realized I'd never be able to do it again, and I really didn't want to let it go. So I racked my brains: how could I turn it into a self-supporting, profitable venture? Out of that came the concept of the Carnegie Club.

It was based on the St James's Club in central London, a building for which de Savary could gain only residential permission, and which became a private members' club, with accommodation:

> It was a real struggle to get it going, but we were profitable in the second year. We're very profitable this year, and many people from around the world enjoy it. We had some luck, and we had a good idea, and we've worked hard to get it established.

Jack Rowell – Rowell the rugby player, injured young after playing for Hartlepool Rovers, at Oxford University and Gosforth – arrived at Bath Rugby Union Football Club when his (paid) career brought him to the South West. He had been manager of Gosforth. He walked into Bath's ground prepared to tell them what he could do for them. 'Bath was a cosy, very conservative, perhaps, sleepy rugby team which had a hugely attractive fixture list in the West Country, but with access to South Wales and the big teams there.

> They were a very friendly club, but they weren't particularly ambitious to do anything. It was a matter of coming from Gosforth, where we'd won the national knockout, and writing and saying I'd like to be involved – not with the idea of taking over anything. I got a polite letter back saying, 'We have enough coaches, thank you Mr Rowell.' A bit later on they wrote and said, 'Well, perhaps you'll come down and we'll see what's what.' The players voted me in, and we never looked back together.

Chris Wright, who founded the partly eponymous Chrysalis record label, is now also the chairman of Chrysalis Group plc and of Loftus Road plc, the company which owns Queens Park Rangers. He admits to working by instinct. Just as Lord Puttnam (the director David Puttnam) has said that he has extremely good instincts, and the courage to act upon them, Wright has declared that, 'Everything I do is instinctive.' He has also said that it is easier to make a decision over £5 million than over £5. 'Five pounds is real money, and five million is not real. A big decision like that, you make easily. But if someone said, "Here's a fiver, go and bet on something" it would probably take a few minutes to think of something.'

David Lloyd, founder of the chain of tennis clubs which bears his name, hitchhiked to tennis tournaments in his youth and slept on park benches, demonstrating a willingness to get more than his hands dirty long before opening his first indoor tennis centre. 'I wouldn't change any of that – it's hard to tell someone young now to hitchhike around the country, but I did it all over the place. You learn a lot of things and meet a lot of people, and that's a training that you can't buy.'

Barry Hearn's white suit – and his nonchalant 'nicking' of clients from his employer – were early signs of his maverick stripe. Greg Dyke, another man always associated with his south-east origins, exudes an irrepressible sense of humour and frankness. As the *Daily Telegraph* observed, Dyke is especially liked by journalists for his 'laddish candour': 'He invites the press in, says witty and indiscreet things, and doesn't complain when they quote them.'

Dyke's early progress on the career ladder was achieved both because of and despite the potency of aspects of his character. This is a man whose brief experience with Marks & Spencer, as a trainee manager straight out of school, has only one distinction: the broken biscuit record. Some years later, after politics at university in his mid-20s, and a spell in race relations, he started on a lowish rung of the TV ladder. If it was sparsity of knowledge about the Salt talks which lost him a chance of researching *Weekend World*, it was his ebullience which gained him an opening on the less formal *London* programme.

Leading the interview was John Birt [now Knighted and the director general of the BBC], and someone told me that the person I was supposed to impress was John Birt. Here was this guy sitting in the corner, so I kept telling jokes and he laughed, and I thought, 'I'm getting on well here.' Then there was this awkward bastard on the left who kept on asking me incredibly difficult questions, and when I got out I found I'd muddled them up and he was John Birt, and the person who was laughing was absolutely irrelevant to whether I got the job or not.

Parental influence has its place in the kernel of a successful career, as shown in Rick Parry's father's diversionary tactics from PE teaching, and by Anita Roddick's spirited and hard-working mother, who ran a café and brought up her daughter to be used to graft. But so does what has become known as the *Zeitgeist*, or spirit of the times.

Roddick was a 'product of the Sixties', and in those days no one got married or had babies. This being the Sixties, Roddick had also lived for some time in California (where she saw and liked the term 'body shop', although it was used for car repair premises) and had travelled. She had seen souks and market-places and a different, informal way of selling. When the Seventies came round, and she sought a suitable husband and prospective father of her children, she did not entertain carrying on as a schoolteacher, and looked at ways to survive which enabled home and work to exist in harmony.

Also in the Sixties, the *Zeitgeist* was playing its part in the early entrepreneurial steps of furniture designer and restaurateur Sir Terence Conran. He was frustrated by British retailing to the point of being *irritated* into setting up Habitat, and so becoming a retailer on his own account.

> Habitat came about because of extreme frustration. I was a furniture manufacturer and I had been making furniture for the contract market for hospitals, offices and universities specified by architects. I had the opportunity to move my factories out of London. One of them was called Cock Yard, which seemed the most appropriate name for any factory anywhere. We went out of London to a new town, Thetford, and built a new factory. For the first time in my life I had spare productive capacity, so we decided to produce a range of domestic furniture which was the first of the flat-pack furniture that many people will have encountered, to be assembled at home – great economy, a great idea. We took a stand at the Earls Court furniture exhibition and put our range on display, and sold our furniture to about 80 different retailers. When we had delivered our first orders, I went round the countryside with my sales manager to look at how our furniture was being displayed. We looked at how people were satisfied with it, how they liked it and how it was selling.

He found that retailers had taken his goods because they thought they ought to have them, and that there might be a market for them; that 'this modernist stuff' might get some publicity, and they might sell it: 'It was a Gatling gun approach to retailing; a total lack of confidence; people making marketing decisions on what to buy because they sold it well last year. It was always looking back at history, not looking forward to what emerging markets there might be.'

> We came back from the trip depressed, exhausted, despairing, miserable, fed up. We thought there is really no point in going on making this furniture, because not one retailer had displayed it properly. They had no enthusiasm for it. There was a mismatch of some of our furniture and then some sort of really bland Scandinavian import, a tapestry-covered fireside chair, some grotesque neo-Jacobean furniture. Very few understood what we were trying to do. We knew our furniture could not sell under these circumstances, so we talked about it a lot, and I said I thought the only thing we could do was to demonstrate another way to sell furniture. That is how Habitat was born.

Conran reacted to the age in design as well as in retailing. He tuned into the political and social change under way, and to influences from Europe:

> When I was a student there was a lot of social change happening in this country, a Labour government with Aneurin Bevan, pointing in the direction of a future about which we were all quite optimistic. We had had the example of the Bauhaus in Germany. It believed that if things were well designed, priced correctly and put in front of people at a comparable price to things which were not well designed, then customers would choose the well-designed product.

Conran had an instinctive belief that markets can be created to give people what they do not yet know they want. It has underpinned his philosophy in every area of business, and led him constantly to challenge accepted wisdom in his food businesses. These now encompass stores as well as restaurants, often located on derelict and run-down sites – to spark off a process of restoration – which excite by their mould-breaking styles and scales. Not surprisingly, he was to discover that his hands-on, dynamic, style – perceived as taking risks in the face of proven markets and mores – was not suited to large corporations.

Looking back, Conran's talents and fascinations were obvious from a young age. His parents sent him to a prep school which usually passed its pupils on to Eton, but Conran's mother recognized that this was not the right school for her son and sent him to Bryanston in Dorset, which had a major interest in arts.

> Being there during the war years, we were incredibly lucky that there were a huge number of conscientious objectors who were artists teaching there, so we had very high-quality teaching.
> I was taught by a man called Don Potter, who'd been trained by Eric Gill, and he got me very interested in the practical skills of metalwork, pottery, [and] woodworking. I certainly wouldn't be here if I hadn't been able to actually weld furniture, and my school taught me to weld. We also did pioneering – we were taught about plumbing, building walls with brick, and when I was at school I helped to build a boathouse, a conservatory and a Greek theatre, as well as cutting down trees with axes. My mother and father encouraged me to build a pottery kiln in the garden and have a potter's wheel and workshops.

Curiously, I have a sister (Priscilla) who has practically identical tastes to me. Once, we were in India and there was a huge pile of rugs, about 400, and each rug was different. We selected those we liked – 27 of them, and the same 27 out of 400.

Priscilla is now married to Antonio Carluccio, who owns and runs the Neal Street Restaurant which Conran established.

David Lloyd's father was a tennis coach, and both his parents were passionate about tennis. Dennis and Doris were also unusual, in being prepared to tread virgin territory, and to endorse their son's ambition to make tennis a career.

It's hard enough now to convince parents that children should go into tennis, and that's half the problem. They still view sport as a sport, and not a job. Of course, it is a job, but 30 years ago that was a tough call. But my father encouraged me, lent me the money to go on the circuit. It was really a very brave move he made. Obviously, I had no option really – because tennis was the only thing ever spoken in the house! On Sunday they used to play each other, and it didn't matter what happened, whether one beat the other or they played together, there was an enormous row. So it was just tennis, tennis, tennis, and it still is to this day.

Lloyd says that although he could successfully conduct other enterprises now, it was his familiarity with the tennis world that originally helped him to spot a gap in British provision, and to establish the tennis centres which brought him real business success. He had been managing a tennis club in Canada, and saw how successful they were. Britain had no facilities for indoor tennis.

Fourteen years ago I needed to do something that I was very familiar with. Running the club in Canada, being the manager and having a feel for it gave me an enormous start on anyone else, and there was a complete gap in the market-place.

Lloyd was able to use his experience as a tennis professional, managing his own money and being used to a disciplined approach to achievement.

I believe now that we could run other businesses because they are interlinked. We are a customer business, but at the end of the day you've got costs, expenditure and income, and what we are good at is managing. I think we could definitely go into other businesses and do it well.

Ron Dennis says his working-class background made him 'focused'. His parents gave him the benefit of not having to earn a living when he was undertaking his early, high-risk ventures. Journalists have been quick to link his ambition – not to mention his immaculate, well-ordered office premises – with his humble roots. Dennis made the observation in an interview with the *Independent* in 1995 that acceptance in any other country depended on his abilities, but in this country he had to overcome a class barrier.

In Germany and France I am totally accepted by the corporations with which we do business – Mercedes Benz, for example. But here it is different. I am accepted for my wealth and achievement, but that acceptance comes with the implied concession that I have achieved everything despite my accent. But that handicap, if you like, gave me a charge, making me more determined and resolute.

The playwright Alan Ayckbourn (now Sir Alan) once wrote a play whose outcome depended on the whim of the characters. A change in their fortunes could result from turning left instead of right, or accepting a cup of coffee. Looking at our Adventure Capitalists, it emerges that even those who had clear goals in sight have always been prepared to change direction when chances came up; to grasp opportunities as they arose; to make changes to the game plan. The big idea was rarely there at the start: it appeared on the horizon and it loomed larger – but it was not allowed to go by.

Chris Wright was adrift before a chance meeting in a pub in Manchester. He had been the social secretary at Manchester University, where he had gone from his parents' Lincolnshire farm to study politics and modern history, and was already a busy student promoter, filling a working men's club with students for weekly blues nights, as well as fixing bands for the students' union. But it didn't look like a career.

When I finished my degree I didn't want to do anything else, so I stayed on and got a year at the Manchester Business School (they failed me, by the way, probably because I didn't make the early lectures, but I didn't realize that you had to make early lectures). When that was finished I had no idea what I wanted to do. Basically, I applied to do every possible job that you could. I just got the paper and wrote off for interviews. I had no money and I was living off whatever expenses I could get from the interviews. C&A was one and Marks & Spencer was another. I think the chap from C&A was being kind in rejecting me. He was saying that I wouldn't like the job and would probably leave after a few months, or maybe he thought I wouldn't be any good.

This is how I got into the music business. I came down to London after what I thought was a job in an advertising agency. I didn't know what an advertising agency was, I had no idea. I came down on the train and went to this very austere building by London Bridge. I walked into an office and there was this very small Eastern European chap with a totally bald head and reading glasses on the end of his nose, sitting behind a desk. We started talking and I started telling him how much I wanted to work in advertising. After about 15 minutes he said to me, 'Mr Wright, I think I had better tell you what this company does. We are the biggest importers and exporters of steel in the United Kingdom.'

Despite this, Wright was offered the job, and told he would be going over to the United States for good. He headed back to Manchester and went into a pub next to the Ian Hamilton Organization, one of the rock group agencies from which he used to book groups. There he found Roy Williams, and had the conversation that was to change the course of his whole life.

He said if I couldn't make up my mind he'd give me a desk and I could come and work part time whenever I wanted to, and try to organize entertainment for universities. That sounded like fun. I started doing that on the Monday morning – calling up the social secretaries, asking them when the term started, what sort of groups they were looking for. I turned down the job with the steel company in America and went round universities to talk about groups. I was selling a lot of good entertainment and realized eventually that I was making more money then I would do in any of the jobs I was applying for. So the job interviews dwindled to nothing and I carried on doing that. It was perhaps five years later that my mother was still asking me when I was going to get a job.

Wright's business partner, Terry Ellis (the other half of the Chrysalis name) had been at Newcastle University when Wright was in Manchester, and had moved to London to work for a booking office. The job didn't work out, but Ellis continued to book acts for two or three universities.

Wright recalls the double life Ellis led in those days:

> He would call them from a pay phone at lunch time, pretending he was in the office. He built his business in the South of England, and I was doing the same thing in the North. We both developed particularly good reputations at doing that, and we started competing in the Midlands to the point that we started undercutting each other. I knew we were actually putting in major artists at losses just to persuade the colleges that we could get them the best artists. After a while I said, 'This is ridiculous, let's meet', and that's how we met.

By that time, Wright had taken over the management of Ten Years After, and was thinking of moving to London. Joining with Ellis (who gave up the day job) they embarked on their venture. Twenty years later, the record label was sold for more than £60 million, Wright's empire was still broadly based on musical and visual entertainment, with interests in music publishing and recorded music, television production, sports programming, recording studios and three radio licences. He then moved in a different direction, establishing Loftus Road plc to buy Queens Park Rangers.

> At the time it had become apparent that football clubs were not necessarily hobbies, but were businesses, that could become valuable, that could make money, and with a friend I looked around at what football club opportunities existed. We had a good look around at several. Ideally you would want a football club that had a huge catchment area and a big stadium and a huge fan base, and maybe have potential to grow. In actual fact there weren't too many of those. Then it just so happened that Queens Park Rangers was on the market because the club got relegated, the Thompson family had put the club up for sale, so we had to look at it. I didn't want to buy it just because I was a fan.

Wright later took Wasps rugby team into the Loftus Road fold, and now QPR and Wasps are both based at the QPR ground. Wright's axiom has been not to plan a course, but to seize a chance:

> I have never had a master plan in my life. I might have a rough idea that I want to get to the far end of the room, but I have to negotiate all the chairs in between. You run into things that might totally change your

life. My attitude is that you have a rough idea of where you want to go, and life is a series of crossroads – you might be planning to go straight on, but you decide to turn left or right, and suddenly you're off on a different tangent. The key thing to developing a business from scratch is that you have to be adept and be able to see opportunities rather than be stuck to a plan that tells you where you want to be in a few years' time. The plan is good, but not if it excludes the opportunity to be able to take those chances as they crop up.

Peter de Savary has a similar rule of thumb:

> I've never really known what I've wanted to achieve. I have realized for many years that every day is precious, and [that] one's life is so fragile. I have had experiences from being kidnapped for three days and held at gunpoint in the Middle East during the terrible, difficult years of the Eighties, and various other experiences where I've really looked death in the face. I live every day as it comes and I think every day is valuable and I relish it. I don't want to know what we're doing tomorrow. I've never thought about a long-range plan or strategy. I've never had a goal. I've just tried to do my best every day. I've never had a master plan or a grand objective.

Jack Rowell switched course in his day job – accountancy – after passing his exams:

> I was the only graduate my firm had ever had. I was going to do three years, the others were doing five, and filled their time playing cards and all sorts of things. I thought about changing a lot of times, but by the end, getting through the final exams at the first attempt set me free. By then I was working in London, in Holborn, and the professional environment at the time didn't suit my temperament. So I went into a famous company [Proctor & Gamble] which gave me on-the-job training, and I enjoyed it straight away. Accountancy came to life. I got into what accountants really should do: add value. Working in Proctor & Gamble you were required, whether you liked it or not, to work with other disciplines. So I worked in the treasury and I was works accountant for a while, and I grew up very fast, coming out of university life and three years' articles, and then to find yourself works accountant in a Manchester factory.

Sir Terence Conran has almost seamlessly changed emphasis from furniture making to serving food (in the Soup Kitchen) to retailing (as Habitat became a chain, although that had not been the original intention), to corporate retailing with Storehouse, and thence back to serving food. He has left arenas to which he felt unsuited – principally that of the corporate public company – and returned to working alongside like-thinking people in the hands-on environment in which he feels most at ease. Rather than force himself into an uncomfortable professional mould, Conran's high-profile, charismatic career has been a living made from all his passionate interests: design, aesthetics, food, gardening, and his trademark projects have blended two, or several, or all of them. Conran's most successful years have been when instinct has suggested his direction. He has enjoyed taking risks with his own money (less so with that of shareholders), and backing his own hunches.

Conran sees nothing remarkable in the fact that he has had two, or three, parallel careers running simultaneously. The original suggestion that the Conran empire could encompass more than Habitat and his design consultancy came from a board member, Hugo Haarbosch, from the Dutch bank Mason-Hope. Conran had sought money from the markets to expand Habitat in America, and Haarbosch was brought on to the board because of his interest in and understanding of the business. 'He really opened our eyes to opportunities that could be before us,' Conran says.

Mothercare, too, was brought on board by external suggestion. Its founder, Selim Zilkha, approached Conran.

> He said, 'Look, I'm looking for a buyer for this business. I want to leave the UK, I want to move to America. I believe in your business and what you are doing. I believe that your product design and your understanding of the market-place are exactly what Mothercare needs.' We remembered what Hugo Haarbosch had said to us. We thought very long and hard about it. We were quite stunned by the approach, and looked very hard at Mothercare, hugely admiring the computerized systems that they had put in for controlling stock. We decided yes, we would take them over. It was a very bold step for a very young and relatively unsophisticated company. In a relatively short time, we did make a huge success of changing Mothercare's products into things which were optimistic, well designed, and which actually matched the aspirations of mothers at that particular time.

But no examination of entrepreneurs and business leaders would be complete without the elements we expect them to have: the gimlet eye and, of course, that enormous bank of good luck which has passed the rest of us by. Time to bring on the microscope, wheel them under, and seek the pocket of extraordinary good fortune and the third eye with which they spot the gap the rest of us fail to notice.

Conran has this eye, supported by instinct. His restaurants – now numbering 13 – span the years from 1953, and reflect the sociological, financial and global changes which Conran has so assiduously observed, and the trends he has seen emerging. The first of this stable was the Soup Kitchen, opened in Chandos Place, London. He was 22, not long out of the Central School of Arts and Crafts, and a year down the road on his own furniture-making business, which was then in a basement studio in Notting Hill.

A friend, who happened to be a psychiatrist, and I were sitting extremely broke in the kitchen of the house where we lived one evening and thinking how we could make some money. We talked about various things we could do and realized that there was no place where impecunious people like ourselves could go out and have a decent meal in nice surroundings. He went off and found a place, and I went off and stayed with a girlfriend in Paris and worked in a restaurant to find out what happened behind the scenes. Not that I knew what happened in front of the scenes – I hadn't any money to buy a meal. I came back and said to him, 'Look, we have got to think of something where we don't have to employ chefs, who are terrible people. They're rude, they're belligerent, they're dishonest, they do everything they can to destroy a business. Can we think of a formula that doesn't need chefs?'

So I thought of this idea of making really good stock in huge cauldrons. You could get free bones from butchers in those days, and make a huge cauldron of stock clarified with egg shells. We largely employed out-of-work debs who come very cheap. They were nice to the customers. You could say, right, minestrone soup, you've got to put in a bag of pasta, some carrots, a bit of celery, peas, and there you have a big cauldron of minestrone soup. We built this restaurant ourselves with our own hands; it cost £257.6d, I think, in Chandos Place, just off Trafalgar

Square. It seated 40 people and was furnished with my furniture and I decorated it with big blow-ups on the walls and French kitchen equipment and cane-topped stools. We had gone to Italy and bought a second-hand Gazzo Espresso machine, the second one in England. When we opened the doors, the menu was a pint of soup at 7d, French bread and butter, apple flan and espresso coffee. That was all we sold.

The first lunch time, 40 tramps came in rubbing their hands, Conran recalls. 'We said OK chaps, this is on us, but next time it's going to cost you money. It was very, very simple and very stylish. It worked extremely effectively and extended to a chain of four.'

After the Soup Kitchen (sold to his business partner, Ivan Storey), Conran opened The Orrery in the King's Road in 1954 then, years later, the Neal Street Restaurant in Covent Garden in 1971. There then came a lengthy gap, to 1987, when the spectacular Bibendum marked an energetic return to restaurants. 'I saw that there was a gap in the market,' Conran says. New ventures have followed this route: a gap which Conran perceives and fills; whether it be for the large, clattering, democratic environment of Quaglino's, or the rather austere, regimented, Mussolini-influenced plainness of Sartoria.

Prue Leith spotted a significant gap in the Seventies, after she had set up her first restaurant in the then unfashionable Notting Hill Gate. She had the premises, she had the patrons, but all she could find at the time were boring chefs. Her response was to establish Leith's School of Food and Wine.

This was the Sixties and most catering colleges were stuck in the boring belief that if it wasn't Escoffier – who after all had written his great book at the end of the century – it wasn't cuisine. So they were turning out boring cooks, and not nice fresh food like you'd expect to get in a good house. The funny thing was that in England at the time, the best food was found in private houses, not in restaurants. You could go into any hotel and it would be exactly the same menu as in any other hotel, and reheated food with the sauce on top of it, frozen foods flashed under the grill – awful.

I kept finding all these students were incredibly hidebound. They had no imagination and didn't know how to do things the way we wanted them to. They were brilliant at carving fat into shepherdesses and carving radishes into hand-grenades and carving tomatoes into nice little baskets. They could do all that sort of rubbish, but they could-n't make a decent omelette. I thought, 'Why are we paying them and then teaching them? Wouldn't it be better that they paid us and we taught them, and then we could cream off the best?' Unfortunately, the Albert Rouxs and the Anton Mossimans and the Gary Rhodeses now come like bees round a honey-pot to the school. They pay more than we do, so in fact, what I now do is train people for my rivals! But the idea was that we trained them for ourselves.

Anita Roddick pushed into a gap in a beauty products market which believed, at that time, that the Western world knew best. Roddick thought differently. She had seen it done:

I was a closet anthropologist, living with indigenous groups. I lived in Tahiti with Tahitian farmers or fisherfolk, so it didn't take too long to real-ize you could wash your face with almost anything. So up came the idea that I could set up a little shop. I'd seen Tahitian women whose skin was like velvet, rubbing cocoa butter on their bodies, especially if they were pregnant. I saw Sri Lankan women eat pineapples, but not throw away the flesh – instead rub it on their skin. It was only later that I realized why they were doing that. Those ideas were garnered then. I said to Gordon that I should open up a little shop with the ingredients that I'd seen.

Finally, let's look at the sheer good luck that came at the inspirational stages in our Adventure Capitalists' careers.

Ron Dennis admits to it. When he offered to take on two cars for Brabham, it was not mere audacity that triumphed, but a compli-cated harmony of time, place and epoch – and he had the good luck to be there when he was:

Interestingly enough, it wouldn't work today. But we set a trend, and there are many successful people in motor sport who did the same sort of thing. But the same formulae that have made some people successful would not necessarily work again today.

For gold-plated luck on a platter, we have to turn to Barry Hearn, our white-suited, ambitious chartered accountant who, by this stage, has moved on from moonlighting on his own clients' accounts and has been offered a job with the Deryck Healey fashion consultancy. Light-headed with dope fumes – these were creatives, and this was the Sixties – he turned the company first in the direction of property (losses of £300,000) and then towards fashion garments (losses of £500,000) before focusing on snooker halls.

> Eventually I had to get something right, and I took it into snooker – not because I thought snooker was going to be the future, but because they had some tremendous town centre properties, and they were freehold. I thought if the worst comes – and we were having such a terrible time – we could always sell. It was in 1974, and I had to work in 19 or 20 very dingy, very working-class places. The first time I went into Lewisham there was a shotgun under number one table and two fellows playing, and nobody asked... They were bad places in those days – the Kray brothers used to play at Stratford, and no one ever asked them for table money! The company wasn't really making money. It was breaking even, but they had good assets, underlying strength, and that was really what I was thinking of. Then, while I was planning what to do with the property, some silly nutcase from the BBC put it on the network, and the next thing, everybody is telling me I'm a hero. They were mobbed by thousands of people and you couldn't have failed. They were dingy, dingy places, and they were packed out 14, 15 hours a day, seven days a week.

This was small luck compared with the good fortune that was to follow, in the person of Steve Davis:

> When I bought the company there was so little business I started promoting amateur events to get people to play. The only qualification was being a regular club member of the Lucania chain. If you played twice a week you qualified to play in national competitions which had prize money of £1,000, which at the time was thought an incredible amount of money. One of my incredible strokes of luck was that one of the guys who decided he wanted to be a regular player was Steve Davis. He would take two buses from Plumstead to Romford twice a week just to qualify to be included in the Lucania national.

Hearn invested his own money in the Lucania chain, selling out in 1982:

Deryck Healey, apart from being a great salesman, was also a very fair man, and at this time the company had a lot of problems and I was effectively the troubleshooter, doing the sacking, the firing and the redundancies, and Deryck thought it was a very good idea that I had a major stake in the company. We did a very good deal on the basis of when it's to be sold, if I wanted to sell, that was it. When it came to it we had a very good offer, and I said, 'I'd like to go now,' because by then I was managing Terry Griffiths, Tony Meo and Steve Davis, and snooker was going. I wanted to go into management.

2 THE EARLY YEARS

Graft, grind and gurus

TV-am was in a state of crisis. They kept coming into my office and bursting into tears. They kept doing it. They'd had a terrible time. They worked themselves to death on a programme that everyone said was diabolical, and they didn't get paid that often.

Greg Dyke, TV executive, in his first position of power as director of programmes at TV-am.

We join Greg Dyke as a fledgeling TV executive at TV-am. He has left London Weekend and the *Six O'Clock Show* with a good reference, and the benefit of an important lesson: 'Most of what I believe about management comes out of that experience, out of actually under-standing the way to run things is with small teams, and involve everybody.' He will need to know this, plus everything else he has ever learnt. For when he joins TV-am, it resembles not so much a pic-nic as a playground: tears, tantrums, fall-outs, storm-outs...

Bankruptcy is an omnipresent prospect. It sits in the corner of the room like a spectre. Dyke has joined from London Weekend in the post of director of programming, invited to apply by the former Conservative minister Jonathan Aitken. He has secured a contract stipulating that if things go disastrously belly-up, he will leave with severance of £20,000, but as cheques (and staff) go unpaid, he begins to realize that there is no £20,000 to pay him.

What does an Adventure Capitalist do in such a situation? He (or she) looks to his (or her) gurus for guidance, puts the nose to the grindstone, and discovers a steel streak. The early years of successful people are dotted with inspirational characters, sustained by hard work, and – not infrequently – beset by obstacles, and even disasters. It takes a certain

> character to distil the positive and learn from bad experience. Perhaps this is one of the essential characteristics of those who rise above the rank and file.

Back in London, Greg Dyke is growing used to his staff walking into his office and bursting into tears. They have bust a gut to get the programme on air, and it has been ridiculed and derided. The critical response is universally dismissive. The staff are tired out with the effort, and worse, this may be for nothing, as they cannot rely on being paid. Oh, and the audience figures are awful. How does Dyke recall those days?

> I think it was the most interesting experience of my life. For a year I just lived in this lunacy. There was no management, no financial systems. I got there as a naïve programme maker and found I was running the place. Everyone else had gone. Very odd, but very exciting – really interesting in the sense of defining what you're like and what other people are like. What I discovered is that there are a few people who like crisis, and I'm one of them. Most people hate it. But actually living in that experience was very interesting. One thing you need more than anything is a sense of humour, otherwise you couldn't survive it.

Dyke's stock of dinner-table stories has been sustained by his time at TV-am as it lurched from crisis to crisis:

> Every week you thought you were going to go bust, and I remember one Friday we thought it was all over, thought we were going into liquidation. All the management moved their cars out of the car park and locked it, and all got parking tickets. I'd gone there on condition that if it went bust they'd give me another £20,000, but of course, that was a bit naïve. Where was I going to get the £20,000 from? I started looking around to see what they'd got that I could sell, but there was nothing – except a barge on the canal out the back. So I stole the keys to the barge, and if we'd gone into liquidation everyone else would have gone home miserable, but I was going to chug off up the canal!

Ah, the potholes; the potential for disaster. But at least Dyke had not risked his all. TV-am may have resembled a sinking ship, but he was not going to go down with it. David Lloyd's first two years as a would-be entrepreneur were spent trying to raise the capital for his first indoor tennis centre, in Heston, Middlesex. He gathered his assets – £125,000 saved from his tennis career, and his house, in Kingston-upon-Thames – and staked them both on securing the loan of the other £400,000 he needed.

> We risked everything, and I think that is important if you are going to start your own business, from a belief point of view and a banking point of view. If you put your money into it, obviously you believe in the concept. I think a lot of sports people do make mistakes. Firstly, they do it when they have stopped rather than when they are playing, and therefore the name has gone. Secondly, they are cautious about putting their own money into it. It's all right franchising the name, but you have to put your own money in, otherwise you don't have the belief.

Lloyd's early obstacles included potential investors who had no concept of what he was planning, or how it might work, or of the customers he intended to attract. He wanted to talk about car parking and social classification; they wanted to know about the nearest bus stops. There was a cultural fissure obstructing his progress. Peter de Savary's plight was worse. He had returned from Canada in 1965 to join his father's furniture business in the West Country, but had a row with his father and left. With a wife and child, he was forced to sell his house and his car, and was still left with an overdraft of £8,000. When he started to make money – having borrowed £3,000 from a friend to buy a business – he came up against an invisible barrier that was to dog many of his efforts. The British establishment has no time for hucksters, and flamboyance is not its watchword. De Savary was aware of a degree of unspoken resistance to his endeavours.

> There is a lot more of the pioneering spirit in America than there is here, and there's the difficulty if you are not part of the so-called establishment, if you don't have strong allies and friendships and supporters. It exists throughout the country, in the City, in the Highlands of Scotland, in Cornwall – everywhere. There is an establishment, and it's powerful. If you are not wired into it then it is extremely difficult to make any decent headway. In America that doesn't really exist, there is not such a structured, obvious establishment. It's just a whole lot of people all having a go, a much freer business community. I find that very attractive.

Anita Roddick hit her first obstacle when she went to borrow money from the bank. She took two children; the bank manager turned her down. Only when her husband, Gordon, went with her was she able to secure the loan. But it was limited. She had £4,000 and no more.

> I was earning a livelihood and I was paying back the bills. But every element of it was frugality, which is not part of the set-up for business now. When you get men wanting to own or set up their own business, they want a small version of a large corporation. Women tend to mix what they are interested in or good at to make their livelihood. Money then oils the wheels to push the idea and see how far it can go. Lack of money forces creativity.

There was not even enough money to buy containers for her products, even though they were the cheapest on the market, and designed to hold urine samples:

> We should not have survived any business school measures... Every problem became an opportunity. We only had 600 or 700 bottles so we couldn't fall into the trap of the cosmetic industry, which has put so much money into packaging. So it was frugality. It was the sort of practice that my mum would follow. She was running our household like that, refilling and reusing and recycling everything, so we put a refill bar in. We were filling up Coca Cola bottles with shampoo.

In Manchester, the young Jack Rowell has crossed the country to a cold reception at the Manchester factory of Proctor & Gamble, where the factory manager is only marginally shorter than his 6ft 6in and – at that stage – considerably fiercer.

> The factory manager was 6ft 4in with a square head. And he didn't like me. It wasn't personal, as he told me; he just didn't think I should be there. The first time I ever turned up in his office, he said, 'Don't tell me what's wrong, tell me what you're going to put right.' And there endeth the lesson from life. You couldn't get better advice than that from Harvard.

Rowell's parallel career as a rugby coach – although later in his life – also involved mixing with straight-speakers not entirely in tune with his aims. 'Your problem, Jack,' said the committee at

Bath, in the nicest possible way, just after he had arrived, 'is that you want to win every week.' Rowell's game plan at that stage was modest: survival, to push the club to fulfil its potential.

> When we started, there used to be about 700 watching and in the end the ground was full, and still is, which you've got to give them credit for. Then there was building up on the business side, and I did say at the time to an interviewer that we were in the rugby business, at which point I got a lot of letters saying rugby wasn't a business, it was a sport. What I meant was that even a sport needed managing like a business – not heavily at all, just creating an environment for people who flourish in knowing where you're going. So the game plan was really to build up something that did justice to Bath City and its fixture list, and see how far we could get.

At this early stage in a career, few go their own way without heed or hindrance. One of the great skills of successful people is to beg and borrow – not necessarily money, but ideas, inspiration, advice from those they respect. They are shameless about emulating role models, and generous in their attribution. Jack Rowell's brusque Northern factory manager gave him the axiom he carried through both his professional and sporting careers, and others learnt, literally, at their mother's knee.

Anita Roddick is the daughter of an Italian mother:

> Italian mothers are like Jewish mothers. They just want to feed their kids or to get them married, because they think that way they don't have to have responsibility for them. My mum is wonderful. She's an inspiration to me because she taught me about romantic love. She also threw a bowl of dirty water at my priest... so no way was I going to go into my life ever being timid or frail. She gave me a lot of lessons.

She also gave Roddick a good grounding in the service ethic. Roddick went into business knowing about working, buying and selling.

When Ron Dennis joined the McLaren organization in 1980, he had no doubt that he was stepping into a company whose image had been heavily influenced by the late Bruce McLaren. In those days, what Dennis would call 'the McLaren way' reflected Bruce's character as 'a very focused individual who brought a sense of style and determination to achieving his own personal goals'. Dennis says: 'I can't say I necessarily inherited his style, and I didn't know the man well. He was killed in a testing accident years before I acquired the company, but he did leave some core values in the company. I supplemented these core values with my own style, which is very focused, and thereafter built the company on changing values.'

Dennis's biggest influence, however, is the lateral-thinking master Edward de Bono.

> I went to one of his seminars and he opened a window in my mind; there is no question. Whether you call it lateral thinking or whether you call it anything... the fact is that he shows you a different way to approach a problem. It was a good 10, 15 years ago and it changed the way I think. He'd probably bang his fees up straight away, but if any one guy has contributed individually to whatever level of success people perceive me as having, I would say it would be Edward de Bono. He had a profound effect on me.

Rick Parry's early mentor was his father, and he reluctantly agreed to pursue a fall-back accountancy option in case his outline plan 'to work in sport' failed to materialize. Parry says: 'At the time my father's advice seemed fairly stupid, but with hindsight maybe it wasn't so bad after all... I thoroughly enjoyed my accountancy training.' It was the discipline gained during accountancy training, Parry says, which has underscored his professional life.

Peter de Savary's father gave him a piece of advice he would never forget: 'The people you meet on your way up the ladder are the same people, son, as you'll meet on the way down the ladder. And they're going to treat you when you're coming down the ladder in the same way as you treated them going up the ladder.' But it was a a widow, Phyllis Hooper, a friend of his mother, who started him on his first successful venture. He met her at a dinner party. Her husband, who had recently died, owned a small Dutch import/export business called Afrex, which she offered to de Savary for £3,000. No one would lend him the money except a lawyer friend, John Lewis, who 18 months later turned down the offer of half de Savary's earnings for the rest of his life in favour of £4,500.

When Prue Leith opened Leith's Restaurant in 1969, in what was then a barren Notting Hill Gate, she was regaled by good and bad advice. The best came from Albert Roux, one half of the legendary Roux brothers.

He was a great guru to us all. He said 'Look, it's perfectly simple, forget about the budget, targets, plans and all that garbage accountants tell you. The only thing that matters is that you have six days to make money. On day one, you have to pay the wages; on day two you pay for the food; on day three you pay for the wine; on day four you pay for your own labour, on day five you pay...'- I forget what you pay for on day five. 'On day six that's for you, and if you're not very clever, some of that is for the tax man.' Anyhow, he said that was a business plan, and I totally agree with him.

The youthful character of David Lloyd was moulded partly by John Barrett, who had a dream of producing professional tennis players from the raw, teenage material. He selected eight promising candidates and had an unsentimental view of how they might be treated. Lloyd says: 'John Barrett had a great dream of producing players out of us eight, and I think all of us probably did as well, or nearly as well, as we could have done, from that training.' Later, Lloyd teamed up with the business man Jim Slater ('a tennis nut') to establish the Slater Foundation, which trained young boys with the ultimate aim of producing a Wimbledon champion.

Barry Hearn is generous in acknowledging the help he had from mentors, and the skills they taught him. Tom Blythe, a lawyer, gave him his first big break with the Deryck Healey fashion consultancy. Hearn had arrived to sort out its accounts and suggested to Blythe, the company lawyer, that the company needed a financial director.

He said he'd give me five grand to be finance director, and I said, 'No, no, you can't buy me for money, nobody can buy me' – and the bastard offered me seven-and-a-half! Started on the Monday and never looked back! I phoned my wife, who had a dress shop at the time, and said, 'You won't believe what's happening, someone's paying me seven-and-a-half grand.' You've got to think working class – seven-and-a-half grand wasn't just money, it was 150 quid a week. When my father's money went up £20 a week we had a house party. I had 150 quid a week – unbelievable!

Then there was Healey himself, the chairman. Hearn says:

> My job was to look after the finances but also [to] diversify the com-
> pany, because we were very much a fashion-orientated business. It was
> a fabulous business, and it taught me how to sell. Deryck Healey was
> the chairman at the time and he was the most marvellous bullshitter!
> He was in a different class – very arty-farty. We were a good combina-
> tion because he would go in and say, 'Really, it's so upsetting' – and tell
> a wonderful story, and I'd go in and be the boots. It was good policeman
> and bad policeman. Deryck taught me how to sell to people and how to
> extract huge amounts of money. He was the best salesman I've ever
> seen, and probably is today, because he could make you feel at ease if he
> was going through your pockets!

The icons of the Sixties – Mary Quant, Folan Tatlin, Ossie Clark –
were both contemporaries and inspirational figures to Sir Terence
Conran, and later, the Dutch banker Hugo Haarbosch opened his
eyes to the potential of Habitat and to diversifying. It was the
Michelin Brothers, whose London headquarters are now home to
Conran's Bibendum restaurant (as well as to his Conran Shop) who
provided the early-work example: they worked six-and-a-half days
a week, including board meetings on Saturdays.

But Conran had already been heavily influenced: firstly by his
parents, who encouraged both his artistic and practical talents, and
sent him to a school which would foster them. Then there was his
teacher at school, Don Potter, and then his tutor at the Central School
of Arts and Crafts, the Italian-Scot sculptor Professor Sir Eduardo
Paolozzi. 'He was always saying, "Build up your memory bank; look
at things; look everywhere you go, and select things." I do look at
things and think, "I must remember that". It's important. I go to old
flea markets and see a piece of furniture or a light fitting and see the
germ of an idea there.'

Chris Wright's heroes are entrepreneurs – 'maybe a Rupert
Murdoch' – and his peer, Richard Branson.

> He has obviously got something I haven't got. He started after me, I had
> about a lap start. I said once in one of the racing newspapers, when
> Manchester City were in the Premier League, 'We're very competitive,
> like Manchester United and Manchester City – unfortunately I'm
> Manchester City.' You could probably still say that I'm mid-table

Division One and he's Premier. I'm all for Richard, he has done really well. I remember when he was the new kid on the block. Mind you, I was quite a new kid too, he was just the new kid.

While Greg Dyke, still in the initial chaos of TV-am, was learning little about TV, he was picking up experience of how to handle money (especially when there was none) from the creative managers around him. But only one outstanding hero emerged from this crucial stage in his career: the mammal at the centre of 'the biggest turnaround in TV history' – Roland Rat. Was Roland Rat really the cause of TV-am's transformation?

It was Roland Rat. Once they'd invented the line, 'the first time a rat saved a sinking ship' there was no end to it. People asked me whether I was upset about the publicity I was getting. I said if you've been called Roland Rat's dad by the *Sun*, it's irrelevant.

Everyone who has ever worked for themselves looks back at their early life and recalls the 26-hour days, the sheer slog of it, the midnight oil, the exhaustion... The early years of our subjects demonstrate that few escape the period in their lives when work is all consuming, all embracing, more of a challenge than they might like and, occasionally, humiliating. It is at this stage that the ability to press on regardless is essential, keeping the goal in sight and sloughing off setbacks like the proverbial duck with water.

'Jack, I think you've done a first-class job as finance director,' said the chairman of Jack Rowell's company, after Rowell-the-businessman had moved from Procter & Gamble in Manchester to a Dalgety business in Bristol, and the managing director had left. 'You've held the company together. Profits aren't what they should be. I'm very upset with it. Everyone's saying you're the man to take over.' Rowell waited for promotion. 'But you're not getting the job,' the chairman continued. 'I'm going out to find the best general manager in the country. If you want to run the company meanwhile, you can do it.' Rowell cannot have been too happy at the time, but he didn't resign. He regarded this setback as 'good motivational stuff', and when the chairman's efforts to find the country's best general manager came to nothing, reacted with bullish confidence.

> Fortunately, he didn't find anyone better than me. There wasn't anyone; I could have saved him a load of time looking but... life was good. This was 1980ish. The country was going into recession, and the company just wasn't prepared for what was going to happen. But fortunately, my colleagues felt we knew what was what. We had to deal with some industrial relations problems. The shop steward who had seen off my predecessor came to see me and he said, 'I'll get rid of you unless you do what I want. And if you don't want my way, we'll have another strike and you'll go as well.' Life's a challenge, but in the end, when I left, he stopped the farewell disco. 'I've got to say it,' he said. 'This man's one of us.' I said, 'What do you mean?' and he said, 'Well, the chap's worked very hard. He's a worker even though a capitalist.' And this is true. I'm not a capitalist, but I was a worker.

Rowell stayed with Dalgety, becoming executive director of a division of the multi-million-pound food conglomerate.

Prue Leith remembers the utter exhaustion of her early assignments, and learnt from it. The very first was a dinner party in North Hampstead, when the Cordon Bleu cookery school at which she was studying was asked whether they could supply a teacher to do the cooking.

> They said no, but they had a couple of promising students for whom they would not take responsibility. It was me and a friend of mine, and that was the first time I was ever paid to cook anything. We spent two days getting ready to cook a dinner party for eight people, and at the end of it we were so tired that we took a taxi home from North Hampstead and spent all the money we'd earned on the night. It was a good lesson, because it meant I'm very sympathetic to young people coming into the business.

David Lloyd was already beavering away as a schoolboy prospect. It taught him, he says, that nothing comes free: 'I bought a restringing machine, and used to string rackets for the club members. I used to con some of the pros to give me gut rather than pay for it. My son is actually doing that now.' After John Barrett had chosen him as a possible tennis star, it might have been expected that life would get cushier. It didn't. 'We used to stay at the YMCA at Wimbledon and sleep in tracksuits and goodness what, because there was no heating. We used to get up every morning at 6.30 and run around Wimbledon Common in big Army boots. It was tremendous training.' Soon, he was off to Italy to compete and at that stage, surely, feather-bedded. Far from it.

> When you arrive in Italy at 17 and a taxi driver tries to con you for ten times more than he should, you either punch him or you negotiate, it's a pretty simple task. I think it's very important to know the value of a pound, especially when it's your own. Tennis is a great sport but when you're not quite there it's a terrible thing – you have to sleep rough, lose qualifying rounds, get through to the next week. We used to wash our clothes in the shower. When you played on clay you'd get them covered in grit and the only place to clean them was when you showered. So you had to leave them on, then you dried them.

A terrible start, then? 'I wouldn't change anything I've done,' Lloyd says. In his days as a Barrett boy he was also required to do one correspondence course. He chose book-keeping. 'I've always enjoyed figures, and when we opened Heston [the first indoor tennis centre] I did my own books.'

At about the same time, not too far away from the Lloyd home court, in Chichester, Anita Roddick's confidence had been boosted by the success of her first shop, and its fragrantly filled plastic bottles intended for urine samples. She decided to open another shop, in Chichester, establishing The Body Shop as a chain, albeit of only two.

> They say location is everything. Well, certainly when I started it wasn't, because I could only afford those streets where dogs had nowhere else to go. But there is a real notion of guerrilla marketing. I remember that the only thing you could see from the centre of Chichester was the pointed roof of the building I was in, so I got a ladder and some pots of paint and painted huge flowers on the roof. I used to drip the bottles of perfume from where I parked my van down the street so people could sniff their way to the shop. I also found this bubble machine in America and I used to put foaming bath oil and strawberry essence into it and it would regurgitate these huge bubbles.

Chris Wright, who was moving from booking groups to organizing their schedules all over the world, has great nostalgia for those early days.

> The early days were when it all started. You didn't think you were working, you didn't even know if you were making any money. That didn't come into it, that was your life – you would have paid to have done it. Obviously I was on the road, more with Ten Years After and Procol Harem than Jethro Tull, although I was very involved when Jethro Tull was just coming into existence. You are living with these guys and you are creating a career out of nothing.

> There comes a stage in every entrepreneurial or business career when a glimmer of light flickers at the end of the tunnel. No one can carry on indefinitely without encouragement, whether this be in terms of promotion, excitement or a big contract. At what stage did our Adventure Capitalists start to sense success?

For Chris Wright, it was early, but its payback was not so much in money as in the sheer excitement of what he was doing.

> With the music business there is nothing more exciting than creating a career for somebody out of nothing. It could be one guy, four guys, one girl or whatever, and no one has heard of them, and you build that career until they become household names. Some of the names we have been involved with have become extremely successful household names, but the first group I was involved with was Ten Years After, and at one point in time they were selling out 20,000-seat arenas in the States. It was an amazing achievement, making that sort of thing happen.

By the age of 34, Allen Sheppard had been offered, and had turned down, the post of finance director of Ford Great Britain. Much earlier, he and the former finance director, John Barber, who later became managing director of British Leyland, had arrived at an interesting relationship from their very first meeting, when Sheppard, gauche but confident, turned up for his interview as a junior financial analyst with a copy of his own recently published book, *Your Business Matters*, discussing how to succeed in business as a small trader. It was written with a friend, but neither of them had any experience of what it was like to go into business. Sheppard says now that although the book sold well, he cannot imagine how he felt qualified to write it. However, his brash approach gave Barber and the interviewing panel a laugh. 'They were quite amused by this apparently egotistical guy saying his arrival should be great for Ford,' Sheppard says, 'and decided to give me a chance.'

Soon he knew one thing for certain – he had no fear of numbers.

> The reason I found the finance training useful is that it does ensure you are not in any way frightened of numbers, nor number-blind. One thing I learnt has stayed with me all my life – if somebody gives me a schedule of numbers, without actually appearing to read it, I can tell you it doesn't add up. That was because Sir Patrick Hennessy, then chairman of Ford, made it a fireable offence if you gave wrong numbers, so you learnt to add up fast. Soon you get to the stage where not only are you not frightened of numbers, but you also know that numbers can be highly misleading, and that ideas and people are more important.

Habitat took off almost immediately for Conran. The time was right for 'a different sort of future', and he was enthusiastic about it.

> It was a tiny, tiny business. The first year's turnover for Habitat was £62,000 – if we don't take that in an afternoon in The Conran Shop now, we get very depressed – but it was the right time. The needs of people after the Second World War were just about satisfied. They started to want things, and things that were different, and young people were beginning to have disposable income that they probably hadn't had before in the history of the UK. There were garlic presses, but they were in France. Chicken bricks were in Italy. I don't think there was any track lighting at the time; that came after Habitat. We looked as far afield as we could, as far as we could afford around the world for the sort of things which we and our friends brought back from holidays into England.

Anita Roddick, having painted flowers on the roof, was regaled by enthusiastic customers who wanted to be part of this.

> I realized it was working when people were saying, 'This is a good idea', and women – people my age – were saying, 'Can I open one up in Hove or in Reading?' We thought yes, that's it. We didn't even know the word franchise; it was just self-financing, which meant you went to the bank yourself and got the money. We did everything; we put the larch lapping on the walls because when it rained the water went behind the garden fencing. Green was the colour which is so strongly seen as the environmental colour. It was also the only colour which covered the damp patches...

Barry Hearn was never in serious doubt about his ability to make money, even as he shifted the assets of Deryck Healey hither and thither. He started making money at school at the age of 12, when he found a magazine containing scantily clad women – and they were clad, in those days – and took it to school. Splitting it into pictures and selling them off piecemeal, he made about three shillings (15p – but this was 1960, and three shillings bought at least six Mars Bars).

> To cut a long story short, we got ourselves organized very quickly. I took two guys who had all the front. They were in charge of sales and distribution. I had a couple of pounds, so I was finance. They were the blokes who went up to town and bought these magazines from dodgy places. Then there were a couple of fellows who were a bit fly – they were out selling these things, and Chunky Ryan in my class was in charge of storage because he was about six foot ten, no one would go near him or his desk – Chunky would kill you if you touched his desk! It was going terrifically, we were making money hand over fist until the fateful day in religious instruction class – it always has to be RI – Chunky Ryan was at the dentist and the master wanted his homework. He said these immortal words: 'It's probably in his desk.' And as he walked down the corridor we knew the game was up. We were rattled and the business folded, but we made a few quid. They lined everybody up for the cane and I was the last. The only question – 'Have you got anything to say?' – came to me and I said, 'Nothing at all, except that it's just a shame I'm going to be punished twice for the same offence.' The headmaster asked why, and I said I knew I was going to be caught yesterday, so I told my dad and he beat me badly. He said, 'You've suffered enough, son.'

3 FOR LOVE AND MONEY

Power, money, glory: what drives successful people?

I am not really interested in anything else except what I'm doing in my business. It's my hobby; I am extremely lucky. Practically every single thing I do in my life apart from looking at monthly figures is my hobby, and I really enjoy it. The thought of actually giving it all up and retiring and lying in the sun or playing golf appals me.

Sir Terence Conran, designer, retailer and restaurateur.

Anita Roddick has no desk; she works from a table in a room featuring bits of organic bric-à-brac picked up on her travels. She has no airs either, nor designer suits, and she drives a somewhat beaten-up old car of indeterminate origin, which could be a Volkswagen. Of all the successful people who took part in the Robert Half interview series, she was the least apprehensive about the reactions of her audience (which consisted largely of accountants and managers who, while they may well buy The Body Shop products, are generally people of a fairly conventional bent). That was what she thought: they liked it or they didn't, and if they didn't, it would make no difference to what she believed or to her determination to do her small bit to change the world.

Roddick and her husband, Gordon – a marriage of complementary natures, hers volatile and energetic, his calmer and methodical – have made a fortune amounting to millions and live a lifestyle that all but ignores it. It would be untrue to align their *modus vivendi* to poverty – for Roddick uses her means to pursue her ethical interests all round the world – but it bears no resemblance to the conspicuous consumption more often associated with amassing such riches. But it is obvious that acquiring money, and what it can buy, has not been Anita Roddick's motivation in building up The Body Shop empire.

Once she had secured a living for herself and her children – the reason she set up the first shop in Brighton, near Littlehampton, still her home and the address of the unconventional headquarters of The Body Shop – she used the business to demonstrate that it was possible to be successful in trade without having to compromise personal beliefs, or rely on materials whose provenance she found distasteful. The distinctive, high street shop windows of The Body Shop (always now in the centre of towns, no longer in the back streets) have been used for highly political environmental and humanitarian campaigns. Roddick continues to travel the world sourcing ingredients and products. She still sees the business of trade as something symbiotic rather than parasitic. A model shop runs on ethically sourced and bought raw materials, a franchisee who believes in the company ethos and is earning a living from it, and satisfied customers who vote with their money and like what they buy.

What can we deduce from this in considering the motivation needed for success? Only that Anita Roddick is probably in a class of her own and impossible to pigeonhole. There are many others like her, running vegetarian cafés and natural fibre clothing shops and boutiques with ethnic jewellery – but no one who has made such a success of bringing their operation not only into the mainstream but into the national consciousness. Roddick does have one thing in common with most of our Adventure Capitalists (although not all, and we shall look at that later): making pots of money has not been her principal motivation. To a lesser or greater extent, material success has been a sideline of other factors.

The purest motivation we find is sheer pleasure. Yes, it can be done. It is possible to find something one loves and do it, and grow rich and successful at the same time! It takes other factors to bring about this happy state, such as commercial instinct, a strong streak of determination and, probably, a serendipitous mix of personality traits with which they were lucky enough to exit at birth... but the baseline is this: they love what they do.

Take Jack Rowell, whose career is going well when he moves from Procter & Gamble in Manchester to Dalgety in Bristol. He becomes finance director (and later climbs higher up Dalgety's management ladder). But Rowell is a man of passions, and he has a parallel passion in rugby union (and, indeed, as he said at the interview, a third career in being married and a father). Rowell and Bath RUFC were together for the next 18 years, a period of unprecedented success. They won the Pilkington Cup seven times, and four League titles, including the double in 1989, 1992 and 1993 – a record unlikely ever to be surpassed. Rowell's motivation grew along with Bath's success. When he joined, he says, the extent of his game plan was merely 'survival', although according to the evidence this is not the case. His aims had clearly enlarged by the time the committee was pointing out to him that his 'trouble' was wanting to win every week.

Prue Leith's motivation was also to do what consumed her passionate interest. It had already made her switch direction from becoming an interpreter to becoming a cook. After building up the business to the stage where it had 300 staff and a turnover of £13 million, she sold out to a French company in 1993. But once again, her motivation was not financial.

> People sell their businesses for different reasons. Of course you need to choose the time you want to sell to get the maximum amount of money – but I think the real motivation for selling the business was because I had begun to want to do other things. I had managed to get the business into the States; it was run by our managers very well, devolved, with profit centres, and I didn't have a job really. I was chairman and managing director, but that was only because it was a company, and everybody else was a divisional director. I began to be interested in other things. I had a few board appointments and charity stuff, and I have always been passionate about education, so I wanted to get involved with other things. I thought it was a good time to sell the business and then – this sounds rather crude – I would be rich enough to do stuff that didn't need a salary. Now I work three days a week for the Royal Society of Arts, and I pay them to work there.

Entrepreneurs such as Leith love what they do, and lose interest not when it ceases to keep them in luxury, but when it ceases to hold their interest.

Rick Parry wasn't concerned about becoming rich when he became an accountant. He wanted to use his skills in some way in sport, even if he was not good enough to play any professionally.

His love of sport led him to seize the chance to work with the Football League, as a consultant with Arthur Young (precursor of Ernst & Young). He had already spent three years in the leisure industry, and in his new job was expected to improve the effectiveness of the direction and management; he then went on to lead Manchester's bid for the 1996 Olympic Games. Parry made his real mark as author of the Premier League. Accountancy was his means of doing what he liked; using his skills in the area he loved best resulted in success, and led to earnings of over £200,000 a year.

Chris Wright was looking for a 'proper' job when a casual opening brought him back to what he had done, for amusement, through his university career. He is emphatic on the importance of loving the job rather than seeking the cash. Money, he says, is not a good motivator.

> I always give that advice to everybody. If one is going to be successful, it is because you are doing something you'd do if you had to pay to do it rather than if you got paid to do it. Maybe that's taking it a little bit too far, but basically you must do something you enjoy doing, so that when you get up in the morning you look forward to the day, and if someone says, 'You can't do that any more, you must do nothing,' you'd say 'Oh my God, I want to do what I'm doing because I enjoy doing it.' If you do that, you'll put all your heart and soul into it and you're much more likely to be successful than if you think, 'I hate what I'm doing but it pays me well, so I'd better do it as well as I can.' I think what motivates people as well is the satisfaction from feeling you have achieved something, and being able to come home at the end of the day, or the week, or the year, and think, 'That really went well, I really did something.'

Close on the heels of the love of an activity comes the true entrepreneurial driver: the love of the process. Some call it a kick, or a buzz. Peter de Savary also calls it fun. De Savary has continued to search out deals long after his bank balance would keep him and his family secure for the rest of their days.

> I'm a buccaneer, a sort of pirate and a pioneer – but not a playboy. I love the fun of the chase, I love the deal, I love the opportunity. I love the

feeling of that adrenalin when you're uncertain and you're not sure, and the sheer rush of it all when it comes good and it happens and it works out as you hoped it would, and have worked hard to achieve.

De Savary attacks his quest with such gusto that he knows he will not grow old still seeking out the raw material for his projects. In 1995 he told the magazine *Business Age* that he intended to semi-retire in his 50s (his current decade):

> I have enjoyed it, it has been great, but I don't want that to have been my only experience when I die. I would like to use my experience and friend-ships and relationships around the world to do some other things. Enjoyment and success are not in the amount of money that you make.

De Savary's view is that unless it's enjoyable, it's not worth doing. Once he and his family have enough, he says, the rest is for joy.

> If I'm not having fun, I don't want to do it. And if I don't like the people I'm dealing with, I'm not going to deal with them either. I say to all the people who work with me – and over the years it's been many, many thousands 'If you're looking for a job you're in the wrong place. If you're looking for a way of life you're in the right place.' Because this has to be fun; you have to get a buzz out of it. You have to long for Monday morning, and regret Friday afternoon.

Sir Terence Conran, asked at the age of 67 what he intended to do when he retired, responded as he had always done – he had no intention of stopping:

> I am extremely lucky. Practically every single thing I do in my life apart from looking at monthly figures is my hobby and I really enjoy it. The thought of actually giving it all up and retiring and lying in the sun or playing golf appals me.

Conran set out to establish Habitat because he was annoyed by the lacklustre way in which other retailers were displaying the furni-ture he was designing and making. It seemed self-evident that if he made a well-designed table or chair, they would be be chosen in preference to badly designed alternatives. Entrepreneurism came afterwards.

I suppose I thought in my entrepreneurial way that this should be my career, what I thought I should try to do in my life,' he says. 'I don't want to sound as if I set out on an educational course. I did not. I design things that I like and believe in. I put them in front of people and say that if you are offered these things, you might like to choose them. If you are not offered them, how do you know you want them?

The pleasure of doing what he enjoys has been Conran's motivation throughout.

Yes, I go to Great Eastern Hotel board meetings, which I look on as work, but that's a necessary part of achieving a thrilling project, designing and constructing a hotel, and I look on the creative side of it as not really being work. I'm just not interested in playing golf or sailing yachts. I really don't have any interests outside my work, or what other people would call my work. I'm interested in food, gardening, cooking, and all of them relate back to my work. I'm also involved in running a furniture business [Benchmark Woodworking, run with Sean Sutcliffe in the grounds of his home] and most people would think it mad to have something at home that is obviously work, but to me, it is a huge pleasure.

The most idiosyncratic elements of motivation of all our subjects come together in Lord Sheppard. Working class – the son of an engine driver – he came from a family which, although not rich, took a keen interest in his progress and his education. He became an accountant because his father suggested it would ensure a good income. As a young man, he was applied, assiduous, confident, but at that stage, showing few signs of the metal for which he would become known. Then he did National Service, and found that he and authority were incompatible. He loathed it.

As an Army pay clerk in Nottingham, Sheppard reorganized the systems so that a month's work could be done in three weeks. His superiors, instead of being pleased, were irritated that he had stepped out of line. From then on, his motivation was straightforward: he wanted to be financially independent. He wanted to earn money so that he would never have to take orders again. Later, he refined this goal to earning enough money to enable him to become an MP (at that time, he estimated £50 a week would do). Although he never became an MP, he did achieve financial security. As group chief executive of Grand

Metropolitan, and one of the best-known business leaders of his day, he told *The Times*: 'I am well paid and I have been fortunate, but you do not get fabulously rich doing what I do. It's not the pursuit of money that drives me, nor is it the pursuit of security. It's the thought of being your own boss.'

> Some extremely successful people have made their way to the pinnacle by easier routes than others. Conran had been poor by his own standards when he and his friends hit on the idea of the Soup Kitchen; Leith had had to deploy comparatively meagre resources to start her catering business; Lloyd had to sleep on benches during his tennis apprenticeship. But they were spared the hunger recalled by those who rose from backgrounds of less material security.

Barry Hearn is frank about money: his mum had been a cleaner for a better-off family with a house on the hill, but her son had plans for his own house on his own hill. Hearn's father died at the age of 41, after being ill for 16 years. It left Hearn with the view that life is short, and not to be lived with caution, and that wealth is pleasant to have, and should be spent with pleasure in case fate jumps in to stop the process. In his early 20s, Hearn was already working two days in one, to earn money to set up his own practice. But when he found himself in clover, as part-owner of a chain of snooker halls bought as real estate but swept along by a boom caused by television, his assets were in a different league.

> I have always liked to make money, you know. I think basically I would describe myself as a man's man. We like to play sport and if you can't play sport it's a sadness, and we have to channel our competitive energy into something else – and I always channelled it into making money.

When he sold out of the Lucania snooker chain in 1982, for more than £3 million, to set up Matchroom and move properly into promoting sportsmen, Hearn's motivational energy was sapped. He found that the money had been wonderful, but that it had come through having aims that were not entirely financial. He had enjoyed his work in parallel with enjoying its spoils.

I was 34 and had never actually had a big cheque before. I'd had money and businesses but no one had actually given me a cheque. It's a funny feeling. It actually takes away a lot of your motivation. I like working. I don't actually spend any money because I don't have any time to spend it; I like working. And suddenly when this had sold and they gave me a cheque for £1.5 million plus, I had to get rid of it quickly, because there was no motivation to go and do anything.

For a time, Hearn's life consisted of opening the mail, banking cheques and playing snooker.

I didn't know what was going to happen at that stage. I had no real ambitions. Ambitions are great, but sometimes you can live in a fool's paradise. I'm a great believer in fate; things just happen. That's the luck of life, isn't it? Being in the right place at the right time, and that's really where I was in 1982, just waiting and enjoying myself. From '82 to '88 was just a licence to print money. I can go wild – I've no control whatsoever – I work for the pleasure of life and the pleasure of being alive. Really, I don't give two shits about anybody or anything else. I can get complacent with a capital 'c', and if there's all this money coming in, spend it, have a good time. My father died very young. He was ill from 28, died when he was 44, and I think he probably taught me more than anybody to enjoy every day. I've lived my life like it and I'm not going to change now for anybody. Responsibility, children... they've got their own life.

In 1987, Hearn could have counted his fortune, dissolved his empire and retired to a quiet life, but he wanted another challenge. At that time, his players were earning 80 per cent of the total prize money in the world, but he could see that the spoils of the sport had to be divided. He decided to go into boxing, partly because he wanted to find another source of income for Matchroom which, by then, had considerable overheads and staff, and partly because of his own admiration for boxers.

I have a lot of time for fighters. Some of them turn out to be little ratbags later on, unfortunately, but there's nothing like a fighter going up, no feeling in the world like watching a kid achieve a dream to a certain stage; you can't buy the feeling. Now I want to be in boxing, but there's nowhere to go, so I have to go and learn the business and I'd say it cost me between two and three million to learn the business at a time when my chief accountant would say in the morning, 'Are you absolutely sure about this?' I stayed the course and I learnt the business, but it was a price to pay. Just the same as doing articles, I learnt the boxing business. Now I'm a good operator. In fact, I'm blinding.

Asked what his motivation has been, Greg Dyke cites freedom. He had tried management for Marks & Spencer, working on local newspapers and running hectic TV programmes. The higher up he went and the more he earned, the more he knew he could walk away. When Dyke found himself out of work after Granada took over LWT, he did just that.

> If you're talking about money, what success means is freedom. I've now been four months out of work. It's all very interesting when you suddenly lose it all – apart from the money, which I might say is important.

Once his finances were secure, Dyke found, recovering his equilibrium after losing his job was much easier than gathering his sensibilities after the death of his father.

Ron Dennis is the manifestation of pure ambition and the fulfilment of that ambition. His clothes and office are immaculate, yet at the same time unostentatious. He admits that he put off marriage, and having a family, until he felt comfortable about diverting some of his attention away from motor racing. Motivation is not only part of Dennis's *modus operandi*, it is also a vital ingredient in his working armoury. It is a force he needs to harness every day. His critics may suggest that he lacks an intellectual background, but he has developed a rigorously intellectual approach to management, even self-management. Every day, when he gets out of bed, he confesses to having a 'pity window'. As his feet hit the bedroom carpet, he allows himself to feel negative. Then he puts this out of his mind and, by the time he steps from his car at the McLaren headquarters in his home town of Woking, Surrey, he is focused on the task in hand.

> Life is full of pressure and it's not always a pleasant pressure. The reality is that you have to motivate yourself. This is the way I handle my motivation, and pump myself up. It is well established that problems become magnified in the dark at night, so I judged that this would be the best time to consider how I would tackle the day ahead. But the moment my feet touch the ground, that's it. I have to be motivated and – somehow – in the four or five minute drive to work in the car I

have pumped myself up. Sometimes it's damned difficult, but then your feet hit the ground running, if you like, and the whole process escalates.

Having won four Constructors' Championships in a row from 1988 to 1991, motivation proved more elusive. Winning, says Dennis, can lead to relaxation on a grand scale.

Believe me, winning isn't easy. Yes, it was hard to motivate myself, but much harder to motivate my workforce. Companies risk entering into self-destruct modes when they're hugely successful. You can almost picture it. The car wins a race and somebody says, 'I wonder if we can win the race with a wheel off.' And it does. Then they come along and say, 'I wonder if we can win the race with one spark plug?' And it does. The problem is that you don't realize that what is happening is a dilution of effort and commitment. The flywheel of momentum is slowing down. Then just at the point when the flywheel has only just enough energy to drive the company, what you lose sight of is that you can't simply turn round and get the energy you need for success at the drop of a hat. You have to spin the damned thing up again. It's not simply a case of renewing your energy; what has happened is that this inertia has damaged the fabric, the infrastructure of your company. And you hardly realize it has happened. Then you have to work really hard to get the flywheel effect back up to speed again.

Motivation is everything to Dennis, as he has made clear. When asked if he could put just one question to a potential team driver at an interview, he replied:

I'd ask him to explain in great detail his interpretation of motivation. He would really have to explain it, and then he'd have to quantify it. And I think I'd have a pretty good feeling. Of course, I'd know his background, his experience and everything. If you've got anyone that you're interviewing it's very, very important – it doesn't matter whether it's a driver or anyone else – you've got to make them talk about themselves. You've got to get them into a frame of mind when they're using their natural body language. You look at their faces, look at their eyes, and their body language, and you can learn a great deal. This guy called Eddie Bowes makes a science of body language. It's quite interesting to see when you pose someone a question how they change their style, how their facial movements change and what you can interpret from it. You're not always right, but if you had one question it would be a question that would make the person unload and talk about themselves. Of course, motivation's very critical in a racing driver, so it would be a good question to ask.

We started looking at motivation with Anita Roddick. Here she explains why she finds it rewarding to establish direct sourcing deals, and what continues to make her strive:

It's having a relationship with a community whereby you can give them more control over their lives by trading with them and looking at them as primary producers, so they can be rewarded as such. We go looking either for ingredients that can be grown or processed, or products that can be made for us, and work directly with the communities. What we really gain, as one expression of Mahatma Ghandi said, is that when you do this sort of work you look into the face of the poorest, weakest person and ask yourself whether he or she is going to benefit. Is it going to give them more control over their lives? Gordon [her husband] has just come back from India, where they make this little footsie wooden roller for us, and with the profits they've opened veterinary clinics. We've just opened up a school for the kids in the community; we have probably the best Aids programme attached to the cities, with elephants going up and down with Aids information in Tamil and in English. There is an Aids outpost where you can get your condoms free. All these wonderful initiatives come from that basic form of trading, trading honourably. We are very committed, even though it is quite small scale, to looking at sourcing all our major raw ingredients, from cocoa butter to castor oil, in that way, whether with co-operatives or just having direct contact.

The extent to which Roddick eschews financial motivation is clear when she talks about refusing to diversify into other products.

Should we go in to maximize the profits for the shareholders? Absolutely not. Our responsibility is to keep the company style and image and integrity absolutely there. I could go into vitamins, but why? Everybody else is doing it. I think the real entrepreneurship has to come with how we do our communications. We have a very mature market here in this country – what next? We're certainly not going to go into the department store or Boots, because that is a distribution line we don't want to get involved with. We're jumping over that and going directly into Body Shop Direct. The results have been extraordinary: women want to work on their own and they want to earn an income. Two, there is an immense loneliness out there, and any group, product, or marketing idea that will counteract loneliness will have a business to last for a longer time. We have stories and credibility and they love getting connected with the campaigns and the social issues.

So what drives successful people? Is it power? The process? Money? As usual, the concoction is not a fixed formula. But although some of our subjects take a more vivacious interest in wealth than others, and list it among their major motivational factors, it fails when it stands alone. It has its part to play in power – for it buys the possibility of release – apart from being in evidence in sufficient quantities, it has little part to play in the process. Money can motivate the executives of the process, but loses its potency to motivate the dynamo. The process itself is the most important element in motivation.

4 OUTSIDE INTERFERENCE

Do the 'experts' know what they're talking about?

I'm not a great believer in audited accounts, I have to say... the minute the accountant opens his mouth and tells me how much we're losing, I want to brain him. Bankers are just cold-blooded fish sitting at the top of some bloody great building looking at statistics, with handbooks.

Peter de Savary, entrepreneur.

Is it intuition, inspiration and gut feeling that convinces a successful operator to set off along a particular path? And to pursue it through thick and thin once the decision has been made? Or are they advised, encouraged, discouraged, informed and protected by their army of accountants, bankers, marketing specialists, lawyers, and City analysts? Not to mention the unsolicited opinions of journalists? What part have the 'experts' played in the histories of the Adventure Capitalists?

Peter de Savary likes his accountant. He must do. The man was sitting in the room, along with de Savary's wife, mother and two daughters, when the entrepreneur was asked to expound on how much advice he was prepared to take. But there is de Savary's accountant (who is evidently not a bad sort, and possibly the exception to de Savary's rule) and then there are accountants. And bankers. And people in the City – the cohorts whom de Savary has never encountered as individuals, only as generic types. But it is reasonable to say that he speaks for practically all the subjects when he says that none of these is likely to hit the top of his Christmas card list.

Accountants – as Robert Half International would instantly attest – are wonderful people. So why are they gathered into this fold of professional *personae non grata*? And what has a banker ever done to Anita Roddick to make her eyes narrow, and her lips curl back over her teeth?

The Adventure Capitalists are so voluble on the subject of professional advice, solicited and otherwise, that it seems simpler to let them explain for themselves. The more pronounced their entrepreneurial streak (de Savary, Roddick, Chris Wright), the more expansive the gesture with which they consign whole professions to the waste bin of honest trade.

In the following passages the subjects hold forth on the reasons for their negative feelings, which are summed up in the boxes. It should be made clear that these are not totally universal. In the interests of balance, there are some almost pleasant comments included. The comments at the top of the quoted paragraphs are the narrator's broad summary of the views of the subjects... occasionally taking a touch of verbal licence.

Banks, Market Research and Other 'Expertise': A Help or or a Hindrance?

> Bankers are sad people so dominated by head office that they are incapable of forming relationships with their customers.

Chris Wright, on whether the business climate is more conducive to starting up an enterprise now than when he started in the Sixties:

> Business climates didn't figure on my agenda at the time. I was doing what I was doing. It is always difficult to start a new business and it is specially difficult to get the money to start a new business. If you have a great idea and you can sell your idea to somebody, hopefully you can find somebody who is prepared to listen to that. I do think it is difficult to get money out of banks these days.

When I started Chrysalis I signed a personal guarantee which nobody in his right mind, certainly nobody over the age of 25, would sign then, but I had a local bank manager [at Welwyn Garden City] who was supportive, and allowed us to do that. Nowadays it's difficult to get any bank to lend any money unless you have three times the cover, or something like that. The way the banks are structured, the friendly local bank manager doesn't exist, it's all filtered through the business centre, and they try to take those decisions away. In today's climate, the friendly local bank manager who made the difference to Chrysalis being able to exist or not exist wouldn't be there, wouldn't be able to go out on a limb to the tune of £5,000, even with a personal guarantee.

At Chrysalis I am trying to create a fund which can be a vehicle to take the place of that friendly local bank manager, because I'm very much aware that he doesn't exist any longer. We want to create a fund for people with ideas for new businesses, where we can say we would lend them the money to start it, and in return, take an equity stake. It sounds a bit like a venture capitalist, but even the venture capitalists these days are harder to get money out of.

Peter de Savary on how banks are governed by inflexible rules and discretion is virtually outlawed:

The banks in today's world have lost the meaning of relationships. There is no such thing as relationship banking. A lot of the great achievements of this country over the last couple of hundred years have been due to the importance of banks. It's not just that they have the money and lend the money, and take their security. They've entered into relationships with their customers. Where the people know the people, there's some real understanding, and therefore the banks, by and large over the years, have had better judgement. Because they knew their customer well, and there has been a better relationship to go through the good and bad times. I regret very much that banking today, by and large, has lost the sensitivity of human relationships... Even though you may have somebody you're dealing with in the bank, the people move so quickly, positions change, that it's very hard to talk to the man who really makes the decision. You're dealing with a faceless machine, which makes it very difficult for entrepreneurs like me to manage that well.

> Market research can be not just misleading, but disastrous for people who work on instinct.

Sir Terence Conran on whether he did market research before he set up Habitat:

> Yes, with our heads and our guts and our friends and our general feeling. We – and a few other people like us, people like Mary Quant, Folan Tatlin, Ossie Clark – started to do things in a different and entrepreneurial way. All seemed to be pointing to a different sort of future and we were very enthusiastic about it.

Had he changed his methods later in his career, when the Habitat empire took in Mothercare, then merged with BhS (British Home Stores), and invested in formal market research?

> Yes, too much of it. One of the things that actually went wrong with Habitat in the Eighties was that I was not hands-on in the business any longer. Other people were running it, professional managers. They believed, and were probably right in believing, that they should get a lot of market research. Market research was taking them in certain directions that I certainly would not have taken them.

What were perhaps Conran's lowest moments came when Storehouse was threatened by a barrage of takeover bids, which led to his retirement from the company in 1990:

> With hindsight, if I had taken the Mountleigh bid, it would never have happened. Black Monday occurred between the time that Mountleigh had made an offer of 445p a share and the time they had to go to their shareholders and get permission to honour the bid. So it would not have gone through – the shareholders would have certainly rejected the bid. Should we have taken the bid at 445p? There were several people within the business who believed it was a good opportunity. We had the best advisers, the merchant bankers, several of them who said it was not enough. That was their advice to the board, which we paid dearly for. They said we should be asking for 525p. That was the price we could put before our shareholders. These are difficult problems. What is a board to do in these circumstances? Does it ignore the advice of its advisers and go to its shareholders and say, we believe you should accept this bid, but our advisers tell us it is not enough?

> In 1991, Conran's Le Pont de la Tour at Butlers Wharf, next to Tower
> Bridge, was criticized for its location; in 1993, when he opened the 300-
> seat Quaglino's in St James's during the depths of the recession, he was
> accused of commercial madness. Neither of these projects was done
> with the benefit of market research.

No. I am mad, you see. If an estate agent says you cannot do something
there, then you know that you should. Marylebone High Street [loca-
tion of The Orrery restaurant] was a fairly deserted part of London. The
Howard de Walden Estate offered a completely derelict building and
we did a deal on it at a very low price because they saw that our repre-
sentation there would help to regenerate the area. Within a year, the
value of the property in that area had gone up by 25 per cent, and
exactly the same happened in the King's Road. At Butlers Wharf I was
told that I could never make a success of restaurants on the south side
of the river. But I had a belief, I suppose, that if you have an interesting
location, and do something very well and with total conviction, then
you can change people's opinion about that place and that destination.
Whilst the normal retailer would say, 'location, location, location' I take
a contrary view, and say that as a private company, I am prepared to
take the risk and see if we can make a success of this destination. I have
had this philosophy from the beginning, from when we established the
first Habitat on the Fulham Road. I have been amazed at how fast
Butlers Wharf has happened; it was a totally derelict site.

And on the only best way of taking advice:

What I most enjoy is a dialogue between people I admire. I think I'm
quite good at listening to what they have to say if they've something
worth saying. For example, I would discuss with the chef of a new project the type of restaurant we were thinking of opening, and say why
I've asked them to come up and talk to us. Then I will want to hear how
they respond to that and what their ideas are. Over a period of time,
about a year before the restaurant opens, there is a continuous dialogue
going on where I'm putting in ideas, they're putting in ideas, until we
come to a conclusion about how it should be.

Greg Dyke on the rocky, early days of TV-am, when money for
wages was in short supply and the management never knew
whether they might arrive to find the bailiffs in occupation but

when, by the skin of his teeth, he and his team managed to propel viewing figures from 200,000 to 1.5 million. Did market research play a part?

> No. Market research required you to pay people – if you couldn't pay them, how could you have market research? They stopped the newspapers – this was a news operation and they stopped the newspapers! We couldn't pay the paper bill. A guy turned up one day during the show and said he was from the electricity board, and we had half an hour before we were cut off. This was during a live show!
>
> It was all done on instinct. We put together a team, Nick Owen and Anne Diamond, John Stapleton, in four days. We just phoned people. When I look at all the research we now do on our shows and the agonizing that was just thrown together. And then trying to take the presenters when they came, and convince them they were a family. Of course, most presenters in those circumstances try to knife each other, basically. Their interest is in being better than the other one, and in why they didn't get that interview. If you can create them as a family, it will work.

> Consultants turn a trade into a science, overcomplicate the business of trading, and insist on such a welter of information that the law of diminishing returns begins to apply.

Anita Roddick on the simplicity of retailing, and why no business school would have been able to understand The Body Shop:

> We were creating an atmosphere that was so eccentric but so right at the time. I had never been to business school – remember I'm an Italian immigrant so I knew about the work ethic, and I knew about service because I was brought up in my mum's café, but there was no business training. Business now seems like financial science rather than the notion of this delicious trading. Buying and selling is sort of out of the window, to a degree. I didn't understand anything and I think that naïvety gave rise to an immense amount of creativity.

On her irritation with business-speak:

> My business isn't rocket fuel. It's just a super sense of having an idea and pushing that same idea without diluting it – keeping it pure, not being pushed into the financial-speak of diversification. It's not diffi-

cult. The financial press either can't add up or can't write, and most can't do both. They try to make this case for business being far more of a science than it is.

Prue Leith, who served for five years on the British Rail board, on two approaches to market research:

The board said they had to get away from white bread sandwiches with cheese, and said they should have a brown bread sandwich. They said, 'We do nothing without market research!' My idea of market research would have been to take a tray of sandwiches round – some nice sandwiches and some of BR's old sandwiches, and ask people which they preferred. They didn't do that. They hired an army of people who asked things like, 'When did you last buy a British Rail sandwich?' and what the flavour was. They filled clipboards full of information and – guess what? – it proved totally inconclusive. I finally managed to get them to agree to a trial of a wholemeal sandwich with salami and cheese and lettuce on Paddington Station. They said, 'Oh, never sell, never sell.' We put out half of these sandwiches and half the white bread cheese sandwiches and 80 per cent of the sales were salami. I was hugely vindicated, then they let me loose with a whole lot more than sandwiches.

Prue Leith on how she built up her Good Food business to a turnover of £13 million, with 300 staff, without the aid of a business plan:

When I sold the company, I'd never had a business plan, a target, a budget in my life. We've only been computerized for a couple of years, and I have to say that even now, I'm not totally convinced... I think there's an obsession with spreadsheets, and with having much more information than you need. When I sold my business I knew on the Tuesday of the following week exactly what the group's profits were for the past week. Any of our business managers could have told you on any day what yesterday's ice-cream sales were. By the 9th of every month I had a profit and loss account for the whole month before – now I don't get the profit and loss account until the third week of the month, and we're still struggling, and we've got 13 people in the accounts department. When I ran the business we had me and my husband, who did half a day a week – there's something wrong here!

Peter de Savary talking to Andrew Duncan in the *Sunday Telegraph* in 1985:

> I try to pierce through things. The great fault all over the world in business is that people overcomplicate, and forget the main ingredients of success are common sense and simplicity. I use lawyers and accountants as little as possible – most of them want to negotiate for you, and then charge huge fees for complicating everything. I get down to the facts, which is why I would have liked to be a barrister.

Anita Roddick on how bankers are ignorant of business and beset by prejudices:

> Nothing's changed 22 years later. It's still harder for a woman to set up her own business than it is to get money for a new car, or certainly a new kitchen. That is reprehensible enough, but it's a fact. I went into the bank with my two babes, who were then about three and five. You never go to see a bank manager with your kids. They don't want you to have a sex life, let alone a family, and they still measure our society's women by how many masculine traits they have. You certainly don't wear jeans, as I did, or a Bob Dylan T-shirt, and you certainly don't go with huge amounts of energy, which is too disarming for most bank managers. I asked for £4,000 and he said no. So Gordon came back and said, 'OK, leave the kids with mum and get a suit, look like a fella – make it pin-striped' and he came with me. The bank manager just talked to Gordon and didn't eyeball me once. Gordon got the £4,000. Hey presto!

Peter de Savary, on committees and organizations, and why most 'venture capitalists' he's met have been disappointingly dull and imaginative:

> Decisions are made – I've witnessed it myself so many times – by committees, and people in banks, that have never met you. You've never met them, they've never seen the business or the asset. They're just cold-blooded fish sitting at the top of some bloody great building looking at statistics, and they've got handbooks.
>
> There are fewer adventuresome equity investors about who can be turned on by the vision, the romance, the excitement of the whole thing. Everybody has so many advisers, there is so much due diligence done. It's so fulsome. The world is such a small place and knowledge flows so quickly. What I call the more adventuresome equity money

that would come from individuals or small funds has, to a large degree, disappeared. Therefore you go to the venture capitalists, who are very structured, very formal, very organized and sometimes rather greedy, and often very demanding, and put on a lot of pressures. These are the tools we have to work with today, and I don't personally find them as attractive as the tools that were available, in terms of lenders and equity, when I started 30-something years ago. That has really changed notice-ably in the last 15 years.

De Savary again, on going against financial advice and buying what appear to be 'unpromising' assets:

Yes, indeed. I bought a bankrupt shipyard last February in Penzance, Cornwall, that had just closed down, lost all its staff. It had been in busi-ness since 1854 and the professional conclusion was, for many reasons, this business could not be viable in today's market-place. I listened to that and assessed those risks and what they said, but I made a decision, nevertheless, to buy the business from the receiver and reopen it and restart it. And 15 months later there are 65 people working there and it was profitable in its first year, and we're hoping to have a good year this year. So sometimes I go against the trends. It doesn't mean what the accountant and the advisers have said wasn't accurate; it just means they are looking at it with a certain pair of glasses. I'm looking at some other additional aspects that may not be relevant in accounting terms or other professional terms. It's a matter of these things which you have to assess, and decide whether to have a go or not.

> Accountants and market researchers may be brilliant at examining and analysing facts about the past, but they have no forward vision.

Sir Terence Conran on the wandering years of Habitat as it was advised to follow the example of Laura Ashley:

Please understand me, I believe that every company should have market research. Where you are dealing with the general public, you need to know what people are thinking. But you have to interpret this, and it is the way you interpret it that is important. If you follow it, you are simply following historical fact: you are not looking forward, and Habitat was a forward-looking retailer. We found in the mid Eighties that people were taking us in the direction of Laura Ashley. They had arrived on the market and they were doing frothy little bitsy things. In the market-place, people said, 'We like Laura Ashley.' The research came back, and was interpreted as us needing lots of little ditsy Laura Ashley things. If I had been firmly in control I would have said, 'No, look, Habitat is Habitat and Laura Ashley is Laura Ashley. We have got to go our own way.'

Peter de Savary on accountants' shortcomings in the risk-reward equation:

I don't mean to offend the accountants. I have spent small fortunes with accountants, and they are definitely more than an evil necessity. I think the fact of the matter is that, to a large degree, they report historically. For someone like me, historical information is really not that valuable. What is much more important for me to get from an accountant is the future. I need the accountant to look at the future. He may use the past trends of previous years; he may look at the figures and the evaluations, but I want him to tell me that in his opinion, looking at it, he can see these forward problems – 'We are going to run out of cash in month nine; if these and these sensitivities don't come right, we're going to have a crisis here.' I want him to tell me what are really the risks in the deal from a sensitivity point of view. And then I can assess those together with market risks, client risks, spread of geography, spread of client base, size of exposure, and many other things. So I'm not really interested in what the accountant has to say about the audited accounts of the last five years, because I'm not a great believer in audited accounts, I have to say. I'm just interested in asking them what are the current today debtors, what are the current today creditors? If every cheque is honoured that's been presented, what will the balance be? How much cash does the business have? And what lines are available and where are we today, and then try to get them to look at the future with sensitivity. And that I find very useful.

> Business school is not the fount of all wisdom.

Greg Dyke, on being dispatched to Harvard Business School:

I was a programme maker who went to Harvard, and I was terrified. I thought this was going to be real management – people who understood and had the solution. What I discovered was that the Americans tended to talk more than the Brits, but got chopped to pieces in the first three weeks. I went to Harvard thinking it was going to be 'Aren't we American, aren't we wonderful, haven't we done everything?' but it was actually the opposite, a massive attack on American management. I actually came back and rejoined the Labour Party, which I don't think was their intention when they spent $30,000 sending me there. I went in 1988, just before the recession had started, and discovered that leadership is more important than management of companies. Managing companies is not that difficult, but leading them is. What they banged home to us was one – and two – that short-term capitalism was failing because its competitors were not short-term *laissez-faire* capitalists. Thatcherism had got it 100 per cent wrong, and was aping an American model which American business schools were saying was a disaster. You can't run organizations if all they're about is their quarterly results.

> Sometimes, even a reasonable business person hates his or her accountant, for speaking the unavoidable truth.

Peter de Savary on being demoralized:

The minute the accountant opens his mouth and tells me how much we're losing, I want to brain him. Because he has to do it, of course, he does, but it undermines you, it intimidates you, and you lose the will almost to keep in there fighting. And it is difficult. When it goes wrong it is very, very difficult.

Pain-free alternatives in research and feedback

David Lloyd on DIY market research for his first fitness centre, and its limitations:

It was in my head. We also did demographics. We didn't have our own machine then, but we were told there were going to be 2.6 million people within half an hour's drive, and I thought, 'We only need 3,000!' That's why we stuck it there. It's probably not the best location because the corporate market has gone down, and you have to pay for yourself, but it's still good. We've tended now to go slightly further out into areas where people live, and we've shrunk the drive time to 20 minutes. Now we have our own machine which has the census, and it cross-references ABCs – that's our market-place. We need 120,000 ABCs within 20 minutes. It prints it out and says yes or no, and that stops you driving round the scene looking at 10,000 sites. But it is still a gut feel at the end of the day. Your machine can only take you so far. It can't actually make the decision, and you mustn't let it. It's my decision, because I feel I have more feel than anybody else in the company about whether we do or don't do that site.

Jack Rowell on the starting point for his success with Bath's contented but not particularly ambitious players:

I would say I was really getting everybody to share a vision. That was to be the best. And people got behind that. We couldn't get new players – there were no inducements in those days in particular – and our neighbours like Bristol and Gloucester were much more famous, much more successful. Good players gravitated there in the West Country. But we worked hard with all the players; we had to make them better. And there was this saying going round the circuit: join Bath, become a better rugby player, and enjoy it. They played hard off the field as well as on the field, so it was a lot of fun. And it was a hobby for me. Fortunately, it's an exhilarating life.

Ron Dennis on disruptive journalism and getting the views of his work-force:

When I get back from a Grand Prix, on the Monday coffee break – and we have quite a large restaurant, but still not large enough to contain the whole work-force, so they all sort of squeeze in – I give them a very much blow-by-blow account of the weekend, which inevitably differs considerably from the perception of Murray Walker and often the journalists. I respect most journalists, but obviously they can never be as well informed as somebody on the inside of this business. Their perception of what is going on is not always very accurate.

And finally, someone who quite likes consultants.

Lord Sheppard on the drastic restructuring of the 'blurred portfolio' of Grand Metropolitan from a conglomerate into a core business of internationally branded foods and drinks.

There were about a dozen of us in the late 1980s who were involved in the process of understanding what GrandMet was. We were trying to understand what the core skills were. Was its success just lucky? We had to think through how we added value, or in fact, if we added value at all. As I used to put it privately to my colleagues, should we reshape ourselves or wait for a couple of 17-year-olds or 70-year-olds to do it for us? We used two consultants to help us – not to tell us what to do but to talk with each of us separately. We had to continue to work with each other, so they then fed us back a kind of depersonalized version of what we'd all said about each other. And the fact was that when we started, we didn't have a clear collective idea of how we added value. Within 100 days we had determined our skills, decided what we wanted to do and begun the task that, within five years, saw us sell 60 per cent of GrandMet, and cut down from 28 to two business segments whilst trebling our overall profits.

Lord Sheppard on the value of bringing in third parties as 'mirrors':

We knew the two consultants well – one was the person who headhunted me into GrandMet, so we knew his judgement was poor! Most of us had worked with each other, but quite often not very closely. One of the people was the present chairman, George Bull, who succeeded me. He and I had worked alongside each other for some time- ever since I joined – but at that stage we didn't know each other that well. Of course, all of us talked to each other but it's quite useful to share with a third party what views each of us had. What came out was the fact that we had, partly by historical accident, great international marketing skills. We also had a great ability to turn businesses round, because GrandMet had been undermanaged in the Seventies and early Eighties, and had been growing faster than its management for a decade or more. So we'd had to develop an ability to correct our own mistakes. Of course, if you can correct your own mistakes, you can probably correct other people's, so that helped us on takeovers.

And on 'brain surgery':

GrandMet had good skills; of course it wasn't just the dozen of us we were analysing – it was the whole team. Our financial disciplines were very good. The 'brain surgery' was to probe deeply into GrandMet's culture and its skills and find out what we really thought, because glib answers come fairly quickly and don't help.

Listening to one band of experts does not guarantee approbation from another:

> Probably ten per cent of the City still believe I was on some form of ego trip of trying to buy and sell everything. Obviously, when you're restructuring a business quite fundamentally, it's difficult. It's also difficult to be able to double the profits of, say, the hotel business, which is where GrandMet had started, and then sell it. You must keep up the motivation of the team involved throughout. There are many thousands of people involved in what is a very personality-driven business – obviously, at the start, you should not tell the newspapers, 'We're going to try to double the profits of this business and then flog it.'
>
> Other decisions take a long time. Two examples: we decided to exit brewing in 1987, but with three Government inquiries, we did not succeed until 1991, by which time the property boom had passed. The achievement of world premier league status for our spirits business, by the merger of IDV with one of the other world players, began seriously in 1989, but did not succeed until the third set of talks with Guinness.

5 SKIDS AND CRASHES
Errors, disasters and close shaves

> When I was managing a lot of snooker players there was a phone call from the North East from a pal of mine. He said, 'I've got a terrific footballer, Barry, you've got to sign him, he's a genius.' I said, 'Nah, it's a ponces' game' – and that was Gazza.
>
> *Barry Hearn, sports promoter.*

Good old Samuel Smiles. He was a Victorian who said that 'He who never made a mistake never made history.' He was right, of course. Everyone makes mistakes, and those who go out on a limb are almost bound to make more than most. They come in all sizes, from small misjudgements to almighty commercial disasters, and they come in all hues, from lost opportunities to gargantuan personal embarrassments, passing through economic misreadings, inexperience, external sabotage, style clashes and plain unforeseeable circumstances. Prue Leith once lost a sink plug in a bowl of sophisticated lettuces when she was serving lunch to a board of directors, but it took the British weather to clinch the rapid loss of nearly £400,000 on a catastrophic restaurant in a London park.

The Adventure Capitalists are candid about their errors. From their heights, of course, they can afford to be. But there are times when everyone's plans come unstuck, and it helps to know that can be overcome, no matter how calamitous they appear at the time. Our subjects also have sound advice on recovering from major falls, and for dealing with the doubter and critic within.

> Sometimes, by the very nature of business, it is impossible to avoid a fall, and the greater the degree of speculation involved, the further the drop.

Peter de Savary, in particular, has sailed close to the wind on many occasions. When he was a young man, he had to sell his house and car and still had an £8,000 overdraft, but that experience paled by comparison with his fortunes in the recession. Against his expectations, the slump of 1990 lingered for half a decade, and he teetered on the edge of bankruptcy. Among other misfortunes, the value of the shipyard in Cornwall fell from £31 million to £10 million; Placeton, the holding company for most of his property empire, which owed £50 million to the Standard and Chartered Bank, brought in the receivers. Overall, the company was insolvent to the tune of £200 million.

> [Knowing when to cut your losses and leave] is the difference between actually going bankrupt or not, and that is tricky. I've been right to the edge a number of times in my career, not least in this ghastly recession. I made a great error of judgement. I decided the recession would not last for more than two years. On that basis, we could survive and weather the recession, and we would hold our assets and subsidize them, and reap the rewards by having that determination and good housekeeping after the recession had passed. As we all know, the recession didn't pass in two years – it lasted a good five years, and there were still some recessionary trends seven years later. That proved to be very costly, very expensive, and a great error of judgement on my part, and I should have cut my losses in 1990, perhaps at the end of the two years. But one does get emotionally attached to these things. We were saying about the emotion and the soul before – and then one starts, unfortunately, to believe to some degree in one's own bullshit. At that point you say, 'God, I've pumped so much in and the banks are still with me, and the banks are still encouraging me.' And that gives you fool's comfort, and the result is that you go on. Then you realize you've made a ghastly mistake, and you have to find a proper, decent way to resolve that problem, and cut the losses and swallow them.

Another of de Savary's other grand projects was hit by timing he could not control, as well as by decisions he could not know, and failed to predict correctly. He bought 13,000 acres of 'wasteland' on Canvey Island in Essex, calling it one of the most strategic land masses in Britain. It had a train station and reasonable roads, airports not far away, and a jetty capable of taking the biggest ships in the world. His intention was to develop an 'environmental' town with 4,000 homes, shops, stores, schools, churches and hospitals, but Michael Heseltine, then Environment Secretary, decided to turn it down De Savary says 'I was just unlucky and out of time.'

> Time and place can be factors in business disasters. So can straightforward mistakes in strategy, or calamitous decisions that should have been seen in advance and were not. Hindsight, of course, gives everyone perfect vision.

Chris Wright still recalls the folly of selling the second half of his record label to Thorn EMI. Chrysalis was the most successful independent record label in the country. It brought Wright £60 million, but although it swelled his bank account, it utterly depleted his morale. He also realized afterwards that it could have been avoided by taking a wider view.

> We sold the record company because we had run out of money and because of the situation in America, where the record business had changed and we were losing a lot of money. Initially, the solution was to sell 50 per cent of the record company to EMI, which was a major, and to have a strong partner in an ongoing situation, but selling the remaining 50 per cent naturally followed on from that. Selling the first 50 per cent was a mistake because we had a fruit machine business at the time, which was quite profitable. We could have sold the fruit machine business for quite a lot of money [although] I think the banks would have thought it absolutely crazy to sell a business that was profitable to prop up a business which was currently not profitable... It's always difficult for any company trading in America. In the record business there were two aspects to it... you never knew when the albums were coming, and we were running an increasingly larger and larger overhead. If you were doing everything yourself, you had to do everything yourself. It was no good just having a promotion man in New York and LA, because who was going to promote the records in Saint Louis and Atlanta?

The decision to sell was sealed when Huey Lewis and the News, then Chrysalis's biggest artist, released a long-awaited album, which Chrysalis was keen to release to sustain the American market. When it arrived, it was a 'sniff', the word in the trade for a flop.

Earlier albums had sold seven million and four million, but the third one nosedived, and the sale seemed inevitable. Wright was devastated.

> When EMI eventually took the other half of the record company I did-n't sleep for six months. It was like my life had ended. The record com-pany, it was me, it was all I had ever done. The artists were my artists – when Huey Lewis was on stage at Madison Square Garden, I was there. If Billy Idle was in the studio in LA and he wanted me there, I was there. Basically, the artists were everything. For six months I had nightmares and didn't sleep.

Sir Terence Conran's low period came when he ventured into the corporate world. Habitat, which had successfully taken over Mothercare and Richard Shops, agreed to merge with BhS (the chain store that started life as British Home Stores) and form Storehouse. Conran says his principal error was his failure to insist that Habitat took over BhS and had the whip hand in its running. In a merger, his power to change it was constrained.

> It is not a period of my life that I look back on with regret, but I realized that my real talent – creative talent – was not being used properly. I lay in bed and wondered what I was doing with my life. Spending all this time with merchant bankers and stores analysts was not how I wanted to spend it. I was then in my mid-50s and I thought, 'I've only got so many meals left and so many days left – how can I use them to good effect?' I'd got on to that track because I was having lunch with a good friend of mine on his 60th birthday, in his office, and his secretary brought us some food which was all right, but not terribly good. He said to her, 'Oh Mary, I've only got so many meals left, and I'd like each one of them to be as good as they possibly can be.' And I thought he was right.

Conran planned his departure over three years, and eventually retired two years before the time he had originally planned. He had seen BhS as 'perhaps the last great opportunity on the British high street'.

> At that time, BhS had not understood how to use design; they were lag-ging behind their competitors. We felt very strongly that there was an opportunity with BhS; that British Home Stores was a very old-fash-

ioned business indeed, quite solid, quite sound, with a good management, but really no vision at all of what the future might be. We intended to say that there is a place on the British high street for a younger, more optimistic, better designed, very well-priced range of merchandise for clothing and home furnishing. We saw it aligned to Mothercare and Habitat. The reason I think it was a deal too far was that it was not a takeover. Everything else had been, but this was a merger.

As the merger crumbled, sapping Conran's energies, the obvious cracks in the group fed a takeover fever. For 18 months, Conran found himself backed against the wall trying to resist a series of bids.

We had the best advisers, the merchant bankers, several of them, who said it was not enough. That was their advice to the board, which we paid dearly for. They said we should be asking for 525p. That was the price we could put before our shareholders. These are difficult problems. What is a board to do in these circumstances? Does it ignore the advice of its advisers and go to its shareholders and say, we believe you should accept this bid, but our advisers tell us it is not enough?

Barry Hearn's most spectacular mistake was to dismiss Paul Gascoigne as a potential client. He was in the dark about Gazza's skills – just as Greg Dyke was in the dark when, at London Weekend TV, he had to steer the station to successfully bidding for its own franchise. No one could be sure how much LWT's rivals might bid, or whether the highest bidder would necessarily secure the franchise. LWT plumped for £7 million – against the buzz figure of £30 million, and even less than the £36 million offered by another station – and was awarded the franchise.

Dyke thought the franchise system was ludicrous, and shortly afterwards railed against it in a heavily reported speech to the Royal Television Society:

Never has government done so much damage to one industry in such a short period of time as the Conservatives have done to broadcasting over the past six or seven years. An industry created over 40 years ago has been crippled for no other reason than, first, Thatcher's dogma, and second, a series of unthought-out and badly compromised policy decisions culminating in the recent changes to the ITV ownership rules, made because someone persuaded Michael Heseltine that they would magically enable British programming to dominate the world. The franchise auction was such a ridiculous concept that one can't believe anyone supported it.

Where LWT went wrong, even in going right, he says, was in offering any money at all:

> We should have bid nothing, if you think back, but we didn't know that at the time. We only bid £7 million because we thought we needed to look respectable. We didn't understand that a lot against us were going to bid £36 million and we didn't look respectable at all, so we shouldn't have bid anything. The process was [that] as a management, we were heavily incentivized to win, but to win for the shareholder. We all had to sell our shares, and the great danger of the auction was that a lot of people were heavily incentivized to win. We couldn't win by bidding the most, because actually you'd have no business at the end of it. We worked out early on that if there was a good bidder against us, who bid to the maximum, we couldn't win – or if we did win, we didn't want it. It was not fun and it would have been terrible, which some of them are now. We did a lot of work on who bid against us and didn't think a lot of them. So we decided to bid low and take the chance. At the time, it seemed perfectly logical. On the day we won there was a great party.

If LWT's decision to bid was wrong, Dyke says, it pales into insignificance against the wrong-footedness of the franchise system:

> They'll never do it like that again. It was madness, and they were so arrogant. The later days of Thatcherism were awful. These people thought they knew everything. They carried out an economic miracle: an enormous boom followed by an enormous bust. They were terrible.

One of the most cataclysmic episodes in Dyke's colourful career, which had not lacked colour hitherto, was his dramatic walk-out after seven years at the head of LWT. It followed the £770 million takeover by Granada, which he had resisted. But not, as he says now, resisted well enough. He should have been more robust, rallying LWT's star artists, and less naïve, ceasing to believe that good performance was enough to make a shareholder hold on to his or her shares. The turning point in the Granada takeover was when Mercury Asset Management agreed to sell.

> I would be a bit rougher now; we could have utilized our artists and we didn't. When we won the franchise back we should have done a management buyout; we could have raised the money and it would have only cost £150 or £200 million. We had a ten-year franchise. But because we had already done it once we needed to buy ourselves 15 per cent of it. We should also have seen the writing on the wall and swapped our shareholders, because trade investors have a different view, and they're in there for a different reason from institutional investors. We were fairly naïve in believing that if you delivered, they'd support you. They don't.

> Whatever the best advice from business manuals and management texts, any truthful commercial animal will say that personalities cannot be ignored. There is more room for antipathy between individuals further down an organization, but antagonism at the top usually results in a clash or a coup. Hopefully bloodless. A clash in style – not usually unrelated to personality – is also dire, and realistically, there is no way round it except to choose your fellow lieutenants with care and crossed fingers.

Ron Dennis, a supremely confident man, not given to self-doubt, recognizes that McLaren's signing of Nigel Mansell stands out as one of his 'few business mistakes'. Whatever the working relationship, getting over the tension that crackled between them every time they met proved impossible.

> If I take a decision, it's often a decision that's been reached not on my own, and this was a very balanced decision. I think that it was the wrong decision for me and the wrong decision for him. Two positives attract, you know, and we sort of talked ourselves into it. The problem was in the actual relationship, because we bristled with each other when we bumped into each over the years. His character was very alien to my character. I thought that was going to be a bit of a problem, and I didn't know how far I was going to have to modify my stance and position and everything to get the best out of him. I just sat in front of him and said, 'Look – I have no time for this layer,' and explained what I considered to be the layer that I had no time for. It was very much his public face, his public values and everything. I said, 'I'm only interested

in dealing with the man, because if you can win races I want you in my racing cars.' He understood and we had very good discussions, and I thought that that would be the end of the problem.

In reality, the problem was that he wasn't motivated and he wasn't able to bring the level of commitment to winning in a car that wasn't, at that stage, competitive. I flew to his home in Durban and I just said, 'I think this is wrong for both of us.' I explained it clearly, unemotionally. I said, 'You are not able to give me the commitment I need. That's not good for you and it's not good for me, and it's better that we stop it and we go in a different direction.' In the early part of our relationship we had finalized the design of the 1995 car which was already being built. Despite the fact that he had raised no objections when he originally sat in the cockpit mock-up of the car, the fact remained that it was too small for him. I believe he was looking for a mental crutch to excuse the possibility that he might not be very quick. And I thought to myself, 'I will not give him that luxury.' I said, 'Get out of the car. We'll make you a new car. You'll miss two races, we'll make you a new car. Or make two new cars for you.' And then we put him back in and he still couldn't do it, and that was in relationship to other drivers, not to the fact that we were or weren't competitive. That was when I said, 'Well, it's not good for you, it's not good for me.'

The end was as positive as the beginning. I mean it was a mistake. It was a mistake for him and a mistake for us and, of course, a mistake that lots of people laughed at. But I was impressed with the guy, and I was impressed with the beginning and the end. Of course, it wasn't the result that we'd hoped for but as in any business, you don't continue to dwell on your mistakes. You simply have to resolve the situation. Selecting a driver is one of the most important decisions that a team owner can take. You can't sit around as if you were waiting for somebody to respond to a 'situations vacant' advertisement in a local newspaper. You've got to decide, and Mansell seemed the best possible option available at the time.

We leave Ron Dennis rationalizing one of the great errors of his career to join Sir Terence Conran recalling the nylon nightdresses and knickers in the store with which he merged his fortunes. It was the BhS underwear selection, and he did not like what he was seeing. If Habitat were to go into underthings, these would not get near the door, let alone past it. Dressing gowns were another source of distress. In BhS at that time, the dominant colour seemed to be pink and the dominant style fluffy. Conran banned them. But bringing about radical change in the culture was an uphill struggle:

> They [BhS] welcomed the merger, but then wanted to go on their way. I was chairman of the company and had the casting vote. I did not want to use this. We had to make changes, and there were endless discussions. It was very difficult to make them give up lines that were proven sellers and bring BhS into the latter part of the 20th century.
>
> I used to talk to the buyers very freely about the merchandise, saying 'Would you wear these knickers that look like a tart should be wearing them?' I made them think all the time about their products and put themselves into those products. It was quite effective in some ways, but often a case of them saying, 'Oh, but look at the sales figures, there are all these people out there who want to buy this.' I said yes, but if we were going to change BhS into the sort of business we wanted it to be, how could we possibly be selling that? There had to be some pain to make the change possible.

The culture clash could never quite be overcome, and the match of business talents collapsed. A contributory factor to the friction at the head of the organization was the appointment of Michael Julien, who came with an excellent track record from Guinness and Midland Bank. The two were not commercially compatible, as Conran explains:

> The various attempted takeovers at Storehouse were extremely debilitating. This resulted in my making what I believe was the wrong decision in appointing Michael Julien, and in realizing that I could not make another change to the company at that particular moment. When Michael demonstrated he wanted to be chief executive and every decision in the company [was] to go through him, I was, to an extent, sidelined. The de-Conranization process started to take place, and he started to change all the executives in the company with the help of a recruitment agency. I saw many excellent people in the company lose their jobs.

In the *Independent on Sunday*, writer Charles Nevin described Conran as having been 'bested by the lieutenant he had appointed'. Conran himself went on to describe Julien's appointment as his biggest mistake. In the same newspaper, he said that he had expected Julien – a 'good, decent and clever man' – to be a 'good running mate', but that the situation 'became him or me'.

Conran says all his mistakes have been 'the wrong choice of people, someone you can't have a proper dialogue with, who can't relate to you'. He adds that, 'In many cases, it's my fault. I don't understand them and they don't understand me.'

The other well-documented blip in his largely flawless career came when Butlers Wharf went into receivership, but this, he says, was more circumstance than error.

> Every development on the wharf went into receivership; primarily to do with the Chancellor's infliction of more damage on the nation during the recession than was necessary. I don't look upon the decision to do Butlers Wharf as the wrong decision. I'm quite certain that on completion of all this work, it will turn out to be one of the most prosperous parts of London. It was the timing that was wrong.

Anita Roddick's style clashes have been with senior staff imported from organizations run more conventionally than The Body Shop. International appointments have been troublesome, resulting in several sudden walk-outs. Roddick says that it is difficult to balance the staff's need for order and calm management with the organization's passionate and idiosyncratic culture:

> The real fault is ourselves. We had a notion that we were too close to everything, that it had too much of our style. We knew our staff wanted a management that was a little less chaotic, so we took people from blue chip companies where they have always got a huge support team. You cannot bring in systems, like total quality management [into an organization like The Body Shop]. Where you get true leaps of imagination and productivity is when you hit the hearts of people who are in love with what they're doing. We brought in some people who use very traditional measurements and their exclusive fear elements were coming through. It was appalling and showed me – God, what a lesson – that no matter how wonderfully you think you are doing, or you think your values are, it doesn't matter one bit unless you systemize it and put it in every aspect of the company. You can have one bad scene, one management behaviour that is not badness or evil, but which can permeate so far and destroy 18 years. We learnt a lesson from that, and after that, made sure that the values and ideas and vision of the company were not an adjunct, but in every part.

> With personal clashes comes humiliation – another feature in every successful person's history.

Conran was dismayed when he turned up for work at Storehouse to find that he was going to be subject to a process of marginalization: 'It was really quite difficult when I had been trying to make things happen in the business, to actually continue, when people were talking about de-Conranization.' Shortly afterwards, two years before he had planned, he retired as chairman. Greg Dyke felt similarly humiliated when Mercury Asset Management disposed of its shares in his organization: 'The fact that we had been one of their best-performing shares was irrelevant. Other companies in which they have shares should take note.'

> Lost opportunities also figure significantly on the negative aspects of business.

Conran still kicks himself for missing out on the chance to absorb (rather than run alongside) BhS:

> If we had been able to take over BhS, rather than merge with it, I believe we would have made things happen that much more quickly. I would have been able to say, 'Well, I've heard what you have to say and I've listened to you; I've thought about it, but we are going to do it this way.' You can't do that with a merger.

He has another gap carved on his psyche: 'I suppose the biggest missed opportunity was not continuing with the soup kitchens that I started in 1953–4. Had I continued in catering, everybody would be having a spoonful of soup in my restaurants, if I had not gone off in all these mad other directions'. He may be being slightly disingenuous here, since he has gone on to establish some of the best-known restaurants in London.

Looking back over his errors, David Lloyd gives himself a retrospective kick for not realizing that his staff were his main asset, into which he would have to invest some time and money.

I made hundreds of mistakes – design mistakes, many mistakes – but you have to admit them quickly and change them. I made the mistake of not having a very good training programme. I thought everybody should know what to do. You shove someone in and say right, get on with it. That isn't right. You've got to give them the background to do it. You can't fire somebody if they haven't been told the right way to do it. We didn't spend nearly enough money on training. It was a mistake, but we got away with it because there wasn't a guy down the road chasing me. There are now, so we've got to do it. You can't skimp on training.

Lloyd's emphasis on training resulted in a scheme called Big Service, with 'mystery shoppers' going round the clubs rating them on everything from cleanliness and friendliness to service.

> Bloopers can come from many and various directions; taking the right decisions and doing your level best is no guarantee against external interference.

Conran groans to recall Storehouse under attack from takeover prospects:

We had something like 18 months of this. We tried to defend our position, trudging round the institutions, seeing the same spotty youths again and again. There was endless speculation in newspapers. Michael was beginning to get paranoid about this. He believed that the offices were being bugged and the waste paper should be burnt and people were following me in a car and girls being sent to seduce me. I can laugh about it now, but it was exhausting and debilitating and very depressing indeed and very difficult to actually run the company and keep a sense of proportion.

External forces were what led Roddick to the High Court, suing for defamation. Channel Four's *Dispatches* programme, broadcast in May 1992, claimed that The Body Shop was not rigorous in ensuring that its ingredients were not tested on animals. The Body Shop later won over £250,000 in damages from Channel Four. Gordon and Anita Roddick were awarded £1,000 compensation, and £276,000 towards lost profits.

Roddick retains vivid memories of that period:

I was so, so depressed. It was ironic that at the time I heard about *Dispatches*, and the style with which it was going to be produced, I was stuck in Sarowak with the Penan tribe, trying to get video camcorders to them through the most dangerous areas of travel I have been, with leeches up my bum, traversing ravines, setting up a human blockade. For us, it was a real awakening because we really believed there was some responsibility in the media, and that knocked it. We absolutely believe that the media do not know the difference between a bicycle accident and the death of a civilization. Creeping nihilism comes in. What astonished me more than anything was the absolute lies. You could actually, through editing, turn white into black. We knew when we had disclosures during the court case that this was a sexy subject, and they were going to sell it in all the countries that The Body Shop is in. Our naïvety said, 'There's no option, we are going to have to defend ourselves.' Everybody else said, 'Don't do anything, people forget.' We were so outraged and so hurt. It is not easy sitting in a mahogany coffin, which is what the High Courts are like, for six or seven weeks, and trying to cut through the ways of being challenged by barristers – always asking double negatives; very bewildering – but we had no option.

For every business crash, there are countless skids. When Lord Sheppard took over in 1987 as chairman of GrandMet, to preside over the hotel chain and a wide range of other businesses, he was driving close to the edge. And there were vultures hovering in the wings, sensing blood.

He describes the risks of radical business surgery, changing GrandMet from a conglomerate to a group concentrating on internationally branded food and drink. He was quoted at the time as saying that if the Pilsbury takeover had proved a mistake, his career would have been over.

Lord Sheppard recalls the challenge he faced:

When I became chairman, my colleagues and I knew that the business we were most content with was a business I'd never run – our wine and spirits business. We thought it had the kind of core skills that we had to work on and that the international food business would go the same way as the spirits industry, which, by and large, it has. We knew it would take many years, but we thought we had to start building up our food business. We had two initial targets. One was Rowntree in the UK, and the other one was Pilsbury in the States. Rowntree would have been easier because we could have used paper, whereas we had to do it all with debt in the States, but while we were pondering – it didn't take us that long – Rowntree was taken over. So we were left with Pilsbury, which turned out to be the right decision for us. It was a six billion dollar bid and it was heavily contested, with poison pills and all that type of thing.

John [Harvey Jones] was our deputy chairman at the time, and we went through all the usual presentations to the board on the acquisition and the businesses involved. We've always had very powerful non-execs. They decided to back the executive management in making the bid because they considered the shareholders were not at risk. If the bid had failed or proved a wrong decision, GrandMet would have been broken up and in the very short term, the shareholders would have been better off. John Harvey Jones summarized for the non-executives: 'Do you realize that if you fail as a management team, either to do the bid, or worse still, if you make the bid and it doesn't work, you've had it?' We said that thought had struck us and we weren't intending to fail.

The radical reshaping of GrandMet involved selling businesses worth £6 billion and buying other businesses for the same amount. The sale of Intercontinental Hotels, a chain of 100 hotels worldwide, was described as the North American financial deal of the decade. The board had concluded that it was difficult for a publicly quoted company to gain the gross earnings necessary to survive in the hotel business and also feared a property slump.

Sheppard recalls his strategy in selling Intercontinental:

We reached the conclusion that we should exit hotels – which was quite difficult because it was where we'd begun. So we put the business on the market and I made probably a few friends in the media, but I didn't make many friends in the City. I went very high profile and deliberately said that anybody who didn't offer us two and a half billion dollars for the business wouldn't get past my secretary. It went all round the world about this arrogant guy who doesn't know anything about hotels that's going to sell this and a leading world hotelier is quoted as having said he thought we would be dead lucky if we got a billion dollars, which is roughly what he'd value it at. We then began a sale process, which was not easy, because we ended up with very few bidders. As the newspapers pointed out, we only got $2.3 billion, which compared with a billion dollars wasn't bad, but of course I failed to get $2.5 billion, so the newspapers didn't say it was good price until five years later.

A leading funds investor of a group which, at the time, owned 7 per cent of GrandMet, said at the end of our presentation that what we were doing was quite interesting, but they'd always seen GrandMet as a property play, and that now we were pulling out of property towards brands, at a time when the property was racing away. As it proved, of course, our timing was perfect – some people say we sold at the top of the property peak. Certainly, the property market turned down, about six months after the sale. The investor sold down to 2 per cent and our share price slumped. The City concluded we had got it wrong and took some years to change its mind.

Some mistakes cost money, others have a more personal cost.

Peter de Savary made many thousands of pounds through buying the London casino, Aspinalls, which he sold for much more than he paid. But his mother, disgusted, refused to speak to him.

I don't gamble... I don't really approve of gambling, although for a couple of years, a long time ago, I owned Aspinalls , which of course was a great casino. My mother didn't speak to me for two years because she disapproved so violently. And indeed I found it a very unattractive business, and was fortunate enough to sell it on for a lot more than I paid for it.

Prue Leith laughs at her apprenticeship at error making, which was made worse because she was actually sitting at the lunch table, having been asked to join the board of directors for the meal, when someone pulled a sink plug out of her salad.

This company had quite an informal style of eating and we used to have a salad in the middle of the table. I got my waitress lined up to do the food. I had been quite nervous to be a guest when I had cooked the food, but was feeling rather confident because the first course had gone rather beautifully. Then the host leaned over the salad bowl and started sort of examining the lettuce leaves and I thought, well, he's never seen raddicio before and he just doesn't know what a designer salad is. I was being really smug and then he leant in, to pick up, as I thought, a leaf. What he picked out was a piece of string which he pulled slowly out.

The string turned into a chain and then out popped a bath plug! I said, 'Well, it proves I washed the lettuce!' I prefer being in the kitchen to sitting dining, I must say.

The lunch-time mishap was embarrassing, but a very minor event compared to Leith's biggest business disaster, the restaurant in Hyde Park:

It was an absolute disaster, but one of the most interesting things about having a private company is that you don't have shareholders to worry about. That's the very good thing about it, because you can take risks. I have always been interested in popular catering – actually, it is very easy to do smart catering. If you have customers who've got enough money to pay a fancy chef, anybody can put caviar into crushed ice and serve it with wonderful toast, can't they? What is really difficult to do is sandwiches for a mum on a budget, four kids on a day out. I've always been fascinated by this and wanted to have a crack at Hyde Park catering because I thought catering at the time was pretty boring there.

So I took this contract at Hyde Park and Kensington Gardens and my husband, who is our financial director, used to give me one morning per week of his life. In that one morning every week, he'd say, 'It's a mistake, don't do this and don't do that, it can't make money.' And I'd say, 'No, there'll come a time when they'll love a glass of Chablis and beautiful salad Niçoise on the terrace.' I had this sort of vision of something between the Tavern on the Green in New York and some kind of beach St Tropez scene. I hadn't figured on the British weather, or on the Department of the Environment, which wouldn't let cars drop off at our little tent, and I lost £395,000 very rapidly. Actually, what it did teach me was that people would pay good money for good food, but only on a sunny day.

There were days when there were 13 waiters hanging around this restaurant, and then days when there were 2,000 customers, all very cross because they couldn't get in, and saying, 'But it's a public restaurant in a public park!' – and using the loos. We used to have these huge queues of people, mums and kids with crossed legs all snaking between the tables, all using our loos. You can't stop them. My real problem was that the Department of the Environment had intended to rebuild the restaurant that had been there. There used to be a Sixties solid building on the road near the bridge in Hyde Park. The deal was that they would knock that down, we would fund the temporary restaurant, and then when they built it again, we would come back into it. There were no guarantees – what happened was that they knocked the building down, had a review of the parks, and decided green grass was much nicer, and they weren't going to put it back.

If it is only human to err, it is an essential of success to deal with it – not merely in a practical sense, but mentally. To get up and go again after a major setback requires a philosophical outlook, and an unusual degree of maturity. If unrestrained, the biggest critic, voicing the loudest nagging doubts, can be the individual most concerned. The Adventure Capitalists share a common approach to dealing with mistakes, which is first to rationalize them, and then to get them back into perspective. Otherwise, no progress is possible.

Teetering on bankruptcy during the recession, Peter de Savary found it necessary to scotch his own fear before he could expect others to do the same:

The most important thing I personally was able to overcome was to quell my fear, remove the fear that I felt of what was going to happen to me. The embarrassment for me, my family, my backer, my friends, my supporters and above all, my staff and colleagues, that there was a real likelihood I would just go down the tubes. And the sheer fear of that, every day throughout the day in your waking hours, is really very daunting. When you have that fear you lose your touch. You shouldn't fly the plane if you're a pilot when you have fear; you lose your nerve. You get the feeling that a steeplejack has when he's up there and thinks, Christ, this is the last time I'm going up a spire because I feel nervous. I made a decision which I could believe in, which was that I was going to get out of this unholy mess with my skin and I was not going to end up in the courts of law; I was not going to be in litigation with anybody, and hopefully, at the end of it, there wouldn't be anybody that wasn't still willing to deal with me. Once I'd overcome the sense of fear I felt more brave, more courageous. Then I was able to face it in a very pragmatic way, hands on, head to, and just get stuck in and do what had to be done.

Sir Terence Conran walked away from the mess that the Habitat-Mothercare-BhS merger had become. 'I said to myself, "Cut your losses, kid, get out, sell your shares and go and do things that you would like to do yourself." And this is what I did.'

David Lloyd's rule of thumb is, first, admit you were wrong. Then change it, and do both in rapid succession. Of his early days, he says: 'I made hundreds of mistakes – design mistakes, many mistakes – but you have to admit them quickly and change them.'

Ron Dennis believes in rationalizing his mistakes, and in forgiving himself for not being perfect.

Every decision I've taken has been the right one at the time I took it. But things change. You can live with a decision, or you can change your position. It can relate to business, or to your private life. Only a fool looks at himself in the mirror and says, 'Every decision you've taken has been right.' But I'm comfortable with every decision I've taken, in the light of the information available to me at the time. The most important thing is not what people think of you, but what you think of yourself.

6 ALLELUIA! SUCCESS AT LAST!

The Croesus factor: more money than enough

I had a mate at TV-am who used to say to me, 'They'll get you,' and I'd say, 'Why?' and he'd say, 'Because you're not one of them; you don't come from their background; you say too much; you're too out-spoken – and they'll just get you.' When I made £7 million I sent him a little note which just said: 'Too fucking late.'

Greg Dyke, TV executive.

Money, as our subjects have already discussed, is not in itself an effective motivator. Nevertheless, when success is achieved, it is usually a useful by-product. When you climb into a jet that belongs to you or your company (Ron Dennis, Peter de Savary), does it constitute a memorable moment? Looking back over a successful career, what ingredients make up that momentous moment, that golden period, that shines out?

> The Adventure Capitalists' attitude to great wealth (which most of them possess) is complex. Once there, and not under any apparent threat, it becomes a background feature, against which normal life can carry on.

Normal life, however, evolves... Ron Dennis takes the view that money is 'absolutely, totally unimportant unless you haven't got any'. He refers disingenuously to his own lifestyle, which extends to running a private jet, as 'very modest'.

Although the Adventure Capitalists have clearly made it in terms of possessions, not all of them take this as a measure of their success, although it can, of course, make it easier to attain personal and professional objectives.

Peter de Savary's attitude to wealth is fascinating. Money is what he makes in dealing and what he aims to make. It is not a by-product, but a goal in itself. He may be buying or selling a hotel chain or a casino, but de Savary talks of money and the things it buys rather as he might talk of apples: sometimes he has 2lb and sometimes he has a barrowload. He has, in his time, owned tons of apples and sometimes he has been virtually down to his last one, waiting for a creditor to come along and claim it. 'Well,' he says, 'I'm always afraid to lose money and I hate losing it, but I recognize that's part of the deal. You have to accept you cannot go through life as an entrepreneur and only have winners. You will have losses; you will have failures. And you try to manage them in the best way possible, and you have to go on and have another go... ' He told *Business Age*: 'You can never be an entrepreneur if you are afraid to lose money. It's like being a pilot who is frightened of the bad weather.'

The recession hammered de Savary, slashing the value of his assets. In 1995, he had to sell the Pendennis Shipyard in Cornwall, which he had tried to revive, when its value fell from £31 million to £10 million. Placeton, the holding company for most of his property empire, brought in the receivers in April 1994, when it owed £50 million to the Standard and Chartered Bank. The company was insolvent to the tune of £200 million and de Savary's personal fortune plummeted by an estimated £50 million, reducing him to his last £15 million.

> I never thought about it in terms of how much I had lost. You build up these dreams, you build up these ambitions, you can see the finished product. You know where you're trying to get to, and then you have this realization in the recession that you're not going to do these things. It's sort of like entering the one-mile race in the Olympics and you know you're going to come in last after the first quarter mile, and you feel, what the hell is the point of running this race, I'm only going to come in last – I'll duck out. That was the sensation I had. I never thought about it in terms of how much money. I just hoped to God the money didn't run out before I could do the housekeeping and try to do everything in a decent and responsible way. I just focused on damage limitation, and at the same time tried to list assets that I thought should be kept, and get

them where they should be. I'm always working for the dream and the aspiration and the hope and the plan and the project, as I perceive it.

It is interesting to note what Peter de Savary considers to be his greatest achievements. They do not include getting out of a gargantuan business mess, or making the £50 million which he lost in the first place, but are a blend of the personal and the professional. One without the other is meaningless (a theme we shall explore later, since so many of our subjects allude to it).

This is de Savary on his proudest moment. It is a yachting challenge, the Americas Cup of 1983, and he is not about to win it, but he has gathered a crew of unusual provenance:

I had a concept that was different to anybody else's, which was that this should not be something for élitist people. I find that unattractive. What we need here is a great British adventure. So I went to the Sporting Society and we ran a competition, and took three of the competition winners and gave them the uniform. They were the team, and they represented their country in America. We went to 11 jobcentres up and down the country, right up through Scotland, and got a certain number of unemployed people and gave them a role in the team. We went to the Duke of Edinburgh's Award Scheme and said we need six youngsters who are achievers. We were going to go there and win the cup – the harnessing of technology and ideas – not just the famous designers, but finding people with great British innovation and energy – putting them together in a massive team as a great expedition to go across the Atlantic. We gave it a hell of a go but we didn't do well enough, but it was a very exciting time, great fun, we carried the flag with some degree of dignity... probably for me that's the thing that I smile the most about and feel the best about.

And this is de Savary on the part of his empire which he likes best: the Carnegie Club, a luxurious country club for high achievers, begun at Skibo Castle in the Scottish Highlands, which was built by a Scots-American steel baron. He later expanded the Club to take in Stapleford Park in Leicestershire, in addition to the Mayfair,

London base. The club's particular appeal to its owner is probably that it is a business venture which exactly complements de Savary's personality. In addition to making money, he loves to be the host; he is expansive and sociable, and the club provides him with focuses for his unforced charm.

> I think we have invented a new concept in hospitality, a way to get more than a 5-star revenue with a 3.5-star cost. That to me is incredibly exciting, and people are very pleased and satisfied with it. This Carnegie culture in many ways is a commercialization of the way Andrew Carnegie lived, and how he entertained his house guests.

What would persuade him to give it all up? 'The most important thing in my life is my daughters. Too many people lack an appreciation of what it is to be healthy and have a nice family. At the end of the day we are all going to end up in the same wooden box.'

> Success may be a protracted blur that suddenly comes into focus, an emerging triumph. There is no great achievement, only a realization of great progress.

Anita Roddick relishes the realization that The Body Shop was going to work, and that her ideas were more than a commercial eccentricity. The next rung on the Roddick ladder of achievement was sudden:

> I had no vision of bigness – that's either a psychological problem with me, or it's my survival mechanism. I tend to think there was a real maturation point when we went on to the US security market. Suddenly you realize that people – strangers – were actually wanting to invest in your idea. That was a huge boost for us, but we also realized then that what we didn't want was to be like some of these large corporations.

Roddick is an atypical businesswoman. There is a significant political edge to her achievements. The Body Shop's parallel achievement, says Roddick, has been to avoid pressure from those who want it to develop in ways which she does not. 'The greatest skill of The Body Shop is not to be seduced by the City into diversifying.

We know how to retail, how to innovate. We don't so much have a marketing department as anthropologists working for us. We have wonderful connections with indigenous groups, and exemplary practices...'

It seems pointless to ask Anita Roddick about having lots of money, even though she and her husband have a fortune estimated at more than £100 million. She has rejected conventional indicators of wealth and status. The head office of this international corporation features a lifesize Mrs Mopp in the reception area; there is a crèche, and the staff restaurant has a soda fountain and a collegiate, rather than corporate, feel. Grandeur is not an element of the Roddick psyche.

> Some outstanding achievements consist of that perfect business move; that glorious decision.

Barry Hearn went into snooker for the wrong reasons (which turned out to be the right ones) then turned to boxing promotion for all the right ones. Towards the end of the Eighties, he identified that snooker had peaked. Sitting in a Chinese restaurant in South London with his wife, he rang Joe Bugner in Melbourne and offered him £250,000 to fight Frank Bruno.

> I didn't understand the business at all but as it happens, it didn't matter. The fight was so big I ended up involving (Terry) Lawless and (Mickey) Duff because it made life easier. It was difficult to work without them, frankly, and we made about £1.25 million on the night. It was a blinding night, and when you see the fight you want to see, 30,000 people on a buzz and you're making money, it's better than sex!

Coincidentally, the fight was bought for ITV by Greg Dyke, whom Hearn describes as having 'more ability in his little finger than anybody that's so-called running television, a proper player with vision and foresight'. The show attracted 18.5 million viewers.

Like Hearn, Ron Dennis had not come raw to the arts of negotiation when he struck a sponsorship deal, so momentous, so demanding of all his skills and strategy, that he counts it as his greatest achievement. Winning races is a team effort, but on this occasion he was on his own.

> It's difficult to share because it's complex. I executed a deal of immense complications and I remember signing the contract, which was a vast sum of money. All the handshakes and everything, 'Thank you very much,' all this sort of thing. I had got so much pent-up emotion that I was thinking I must not show how much this actually meant to me. I got in the lift to go down a very big office building and I was a full 15 floors from where I'd got on, all on my own, and I went ballistic. I can still remember the adrenalin running through me. Winning races gives you a great deal of satisfaction from playing a part in the strategy, but that's not the same as the buzz you gain when you make a singular achievement. And it is moments like that, when you've signed a contract or you've outmanoeuvred someone in business, that you get the buzz. That's why I still do it. I love the buzz that comes from the business aspect.

Prue Leith's hard-earned plate bore two prestigious contracts. Her efforts to change the British Rail sandwich contributed to an offer to provide the food aboard the Orient Express. This, along with being selected to cater at the Queen Elizabeth II Conference Centre in Westminster, are part of the litany of her proudest days.

> But Leith's proudest day reflects the mix of personal and professional which many Adventure Capitalists require before they will admit that an event is momentous.

> When I got the Orient Express train contract I thought that was fantastic; when we got the Queen Elizabeth Conference Centre contract I thought that was fantastic. But I'm probably proudest of being chairman of the Royal Society of Arts. Of course, it's not in my field at all, it's miles from cooking, so I am particularly interested in it and I only have two years to enjoy it, but I'm very proud of being elected.

Jack Rowell's professional career, becoming a director of Dalgety, and his sporting career, coaching Bath RUFC to unprecedented success, and then England, gives him plenty of material to reflect upon. But this is what he says when asked his greatest achievement: 'My two children. They're wonderful young men, so their mother tells me. My wife's a single-parent family, so she says. I've never pushed them that way, but one played a bit of rugby, the other got injured, got hit the hardest. When they turned up, that was the best moment of my life.'

Greg Dyke could not put his finger on his outstanding achievement, but he knew that no setback in his professional life could ever pain him as much as in his personal life. Speaking shortly after leaving London Weekend TV, following the Granada takeover, he said: 'It's very interesting to discover how much of me is an individual, how much of me is the job, how much the support, the respect – that's quite tough. Success, I suppose, is how to survive in the rough times. We can all survive in the good times. When you analyse what are the best times in your life and what are the worst, the best times are a mixture of your personal life and business life. The worst times are all about your personal life.'

> We have encountered two extremes in attitudes to money: Peter de Savary who moves it around, makes it, loses it, manages it, risks it, and Anita Roddick, to whom it seems of little importance. Between these two, the attitudes of our successful subjects to money fall not far from each other on the spectrum. They like being rich, but wealth on its own cannot make up for lacking belief in what you do.

Prue Leith sold Leith's Good Food Ltd when she had no more ambition for it and wanted to be self-supporting, so that she could do work for bodies she believed in, without needing to be paid. David Lloyd later sold his fitness centres to Whitbread, leaving because of a culture clash. Jack Rowell, interviewed by Frank Keating in the *Guardian* in 1996, during a period of criticism of his strategy and style as England coach, said: 'I loved coaching Bath for 17 years. It was love and enjoyment, and I never even claimed expenses, let alone made any money out of it.' Kate Battersby, a *Sunday Telegraph* writer, noted that although Rowell was rich by most people's standards, it was talk of failure which made him twitch: 'He is a self-made man who becomes physically uncomfort-able even so much as debating failure. Every principle which has served him in business he has applied to rugby; the two are insep-arable.'

Sir Terence Conran reviews his career, now approaching its half century, in isolation from the money it has brought him. He cannot think of one project he has enjoyed above the rest. 'The latest ideas are always the best.'

He is more certain of one thing: money has not been his motiva-tor. He turned his back easily on Storehouse when it was a £1.5 bil-lion company and went back to running a small group. It turned out to make him richer than Storehouse but, as he says, it wasn't the money that made up his mind.

> The money is absolutely on the side. It is almost like going back to Habitat in its entrepreneurial days with a team around me whom I like very much, who are my friends, with whom I enjoy having lunch, hav-ing dinner, seeing at weekends and so forth. All of us working together very closely. There is a great sense of enthusiasm in the business. I can-not think of a better way of going through the last quarter of my life. I have never ever been the slightest bit interested in money. It is what you can do with the money and the doing of things that has given me pleasure in my life. The amassing, even if it is totally intangible paper money like Storehouse shares, was of supreme disinterest to me. I have no ambitions to die a rich man, but I have ambitions to actually use that money which I have – which, sadly, is not £200 million, but maybe it will be worth £200 million by the time I die.

Conran started the Nineties with a spectacular failure when Butlers Wharf, his development of shops and restaurants in south-east London, went into receivership with bank debts of some £50 mil-lion. Personally, he lost £5 million, plus another £8 million he had lent to the development. His fortune was said to have fallen over five years by £150 million. He was not losing sleep. 'In one way I'm sad I lost money on it, but it was money I could afford to lose. I never had any dreams of millions. My idea is not to die rich.'

His extravagances now are a Wiltshire home which is too big for him (although it turns out to have been an investment), four Cuban cigars every day, good wine, a driver and a holiday house in France.

When I go on holiday I spend the first two days absolutely crashed out, swimming and reading easy-to-read novels. Then I'm bored. One of my great pleasures is to go out and have really good meals, but even then, I could say that was part of my work. If you're a war child, and started your adult life in the post-war years, it's very very difficult indeed to be extravagant. I go round turning lights off and the heating off in rooms that people aren't in, and I hate waste. But that has always been part of my philosophy: I hate waste.

Conran has hopes for his obituary: 'I'd like it to say something like, "He offered the British public things they didn't know they wanted – furniture and food, a style of life." I suppose that's the nub of it. I'm lucky to have had enough experience and to have been everywhere in the world and this is my selection of ideas that I think people might like.'

> The wonderful thing about luxuries, to someone who is rich, is that they can pick and choose like children with a bag of change at a sweet counter: should they or shouldn't they? Is it good for them or not? What will be the effect on them as people? Being as rich as stink opens up a new debate on the acquisition of goodies. It is an equation that involves many factors. Except money.

David Lloyd admits to having paid off his mortgage, and to pandering to his longstanding weakness for cars (a blue Ferrari at the time of the interview). Greg Dyke confesses to a modest extension on his Twickenham home.

Peter de Savary has had cars, jets, helicopters. He still smokes Cuban cigars, and he loves the opulence of Skibo Castle. Interviewed by the *Independent on Sunday* during the recession (1992) he allowed himself 30 seconds of regret. He felt 'crucified' by the recession. 'I used to have offices on three floors on Pall Mall. Now I'm paying £18,000 for a third-floor office in the Cromwell Road. Of course it bloody hurts,' he said. 'The corporate jets and helicopters are gone and the staff have been cut. I've got each person doing the work of three and I am extracting maximum credit. I do a deal with every creditor.'

De Savary had to look to his own philosophy: you can only sleep in one bed at a time, as he said, in better times, in the *Mail on Sunday*:

> It's better, of course, to live comfortably than uncomfortably, but at the end of the day there is only one bed I can sleep in, one house I can live in, one car I can drive at any given time. I don't want to leave an empire behind me. I would rather put people together to do things, and take pleasure out of seeing them get on with it. I would rather devote my energies to the challenge of getting to know and understand one or two interesting people than chase the social circuit... I am really happiest being able to go home in the evening, cook dinner, and be in bed by 10.30, rather than gallivanting around the social scene.

Prue Leith loves tennis and gardening. Not diamonds and pearls. Her extravagance is her garden:

> We have a lovely house in the country and I am mad about gardening. I spend ridiculous amounts of money on the garden. One year my husband gave me a wall which is 45ft long and 9ft high, separating the vegetable garden from the herbaceous border. This gave me a sunny wall to grow the right creepers on. One year I had a rose tunnel and this year I'm going to have a sprinkler system put into the whole garden and build a reservoir. It's quite a small garden and it gets an awful lot of attention for a small garden, but I love it.

Who is the richest of our rich? It is hard to say; there are so many noughts to consider. One of them must be Ron Dennis, who doubts that he is the 254th richest man in the UK (he thinks he may be higher). His attitude to his wealth is interesting. He has not moved far from where he came from – he still lives near Woking – but he nips over to the South of France for breaks, and moves around in a helicopter. He has everything he wants – 'Yes, sure, all those material things' – and has moved on.

> What is very important to my wife and myself is that the kids grow up with their feet on the ground. They're not precocious, and they understand the right values. Their future is secure, but they don't really understand it all yet. We're making every effort to ensure that they grow up as balanced and sensible as possible, which means keeping them in a relatively sensible environment as much as possible. Yes, they

may get used to the fact that we have our own aeroplane, but as regards the manner in which we live, I think it is comparatively normal. In due course we will move into a larger house, but we have pretty simple tastes. The material side of things is not of prime importance.

It takes McLaren's own products, the F1 road car, to move Dennis to any passion about possessions:

As regards how you measure it: I'd probably stand by one of the road cars and look at it. I'm fiercely proud of the car because it's just a really special thing. It will become one of the most collectable cars in the history of automobiles. No one will make one like it. Anyone who could afford to buy one and hasn't bought one is an idiot because they will become hugely valuable. They cost $1 million and probably they cost $900,000 to make. Basically, there is not a huge profit. They cost that because that's how much effort, time, money, we've put into them. They are that good.

7 *SINE QUA NON*

The essential ingredients of success

I'd like to extol the virtue of doggedness. It sounds boring, but any-thing is easy to start – starting a novel, starting in business, starting a baby, starting a marriage. It's keeping the thing going that is difficult.
Prue Leith, caterer and businesswoman.

Profiles of successful people inevitably refer to their personal qual-ities – qualities which are denied the rank and file treading the boards of ordinary ambition. Peter de Savary has charm (legendary is the usual adjective attached) and Sir Terence Conran has innate style and intuition. Jack Rowell has drive and energy. Any more of this and lesser mortals, the non-charming, non-charismatic, earth-bound rank and file, which includes most us, would shrivel up under the weight of our inferiority complexes.

So take heart: we shall come across charisma and charm; we shall encounter the easy power to mesmerize and the possession of frightening energy, but we shall also find attributes which can be learned or acquired. Peter de Savary was probably born with the gift of the gab, but sometimes it is sheer force of will which makes others conclude that an individual is charismatic. Charismatic peo-ple can be those whose sights are so focused on their aims that they are effectively armoured against barbs. Nothing aids this coveted quality more than the appearance of unshakable confidence. Skills bring less definable qualities, and most skills are bred.

As Prue Leith says, let's hear it for doggedness, and its cousins – application, single-mindedness, determination and a refusal to be deterred, distracted and downhearted. These are the ingredients that emerge repeatedly in the armoury of the successful. If faint heart never won fair lady, an ambivalent heart certainly never wins the chairman's chair. As David Lloyd says:

> You've got to believe. No one believed [the fitness centres] could work and when someone keeps saying to you, 'It can't work, it can't work, it can't work' you have to say, 'Bugger it, it's going to work' and you have to prove them wrong. I love to prove people wrong. My own money was in there and my family's money was in there. It was a dream that I had to make work.

Lloyd is a good example of someone who has learned to be capable. When he began the fitness centres he was basing a business on a sport he knew well and an idea he had seen working well. But now, he believes he could translate those skills: 'It would have been harder for me 14 years ago to have done a different business, but the background of being a professional tennis player, managing my own money, would stand me in good stead in whatever business we do. I think we could definitely go into other businesses and do it well.'

Prue Leith has been described as a formidable boss. Her own description of herself is 'bossy, an egotist, a policeman and a nanny'. The restaurant business, she says, may appear to consist of swanning around pouring out brandies to favoured customers and receiving praise, but the reality is closer to ordinary graft.

> Actually, it is very much about being a policeman – making sure the rubbish is being taken away every day, that the yard is scrubbed, the light-bulbs are put in and the loo paper hasn't changed to pink when it should be blue. And because I'm not the managing director and not the chef, I am the ideal person to be the policeman because I'm the one who comes in with outside eyes.

So far, so achievable. And so to Leith's favourite quality, which rarely features in management manuals:

> I am very dogged. A nice Frenchman ran my restaurant for a while. He said to me as he quit, 'I have worked for you for 15 years. After five years I hated the staff, after ten years I hated the customers and now I hate you.' I asked why and he said, 'Because you never give up – you just go on and on and on in that boring way about the same thing.' What sparked this was that I wanted the customers who were coming

in for a special dinner to have the bar to have drinks in, and he knew it would be easier if he could make them have drinks in the room where they were going to have dinner. If we had them in the bar, the staff meal had to be moved a to half an hour earlier, and the bar had to be cleaned a bit earlier. It would all be more difficult. But if I'm good at anything it's thinking things back from the customer's point of view, so I was banging on and kept coming back to the same thing. To have the doggedness to keep coming back feeling refreshed about it and feeling pleasure about it, that's good.

Ron Dennis doesn't talk about doggedness but dogged he certainly is. He knew where he wanted to go and ensured that he got there by doing whatever it took, and he is still there at his desk, pursuing the next deal. Not for him the life of the dilettante with afternoons on the golf course. The hand of fate has played no part in shaping Dennis's career path:

It is not by accident that I'm doing exactly what I want to do. It is by choice and design. It has come about by thinking, 'This is what I want to do, this is where I'm going and this is how I'm going to get there.'

Secondly, I would never do a salaried job. It's constraining. I would not put myself in a position where my performance was directly related to results. I think I could do a brilliant job managing drivers' affairs. Most managers are rubbish and have no idea how to extract the best out of the deal. I believe I could do a pretty competent job at that but equally – and I think that's one of my strong points – I'm pretty good at negotiating and, if I were put in an environment where I was managing, say, a musician or a film star, I think I'd be pretty competent at it. So if I had to choose a different career away from motor sport then it would be the management of some expert, because I think most experts don't manage themselves very well.

Successful people may move up the hierarchy, but they rarely move their sights. Anita Roddick says she has problems in relinquishing any part of her business as it has moved from a small chain to a multinational.

It's your territory and for any founder or entrepreneur, it is really important to have those guidelines. I will not let go on aesthetics. I am obsessed with the style, the image, what the shops look like, the graphics and the illustrations – and the values. I constantly ask of the company, 'How brave are we? Where is the edge of bravery in this company?' I won't let go of product development, which I adore. Everything else, I'm happy to let go of. What gives my company an edge is that I get out of my chair and go out of the office and stay in these countries. It's the real love of the grass roots. I sometimes make sure we have board meetings in the shops. That is exhausting. But other than that there has been very little change.

Application can never be relinquished from the kit of a successful entrepreneur. Barry Hearn, rich through snooker, could have retired and lived on his earnings. In fact, he sold out of the Lucania chain in 1982 (he was 34, and very rich). 'The growth had gone by then, the buzz of being involved. It's a different type of animal that can do the same thing for 30 or 40 years. I have a little bit of a concentration span problem after about six or seven.' His attention span for snooker was exhausted, but not his interest in sport. He decided to go into boxing. It lost him about £2 million and he stuck at it, losing money hand over fist, until he had learned the trade.

Lord Sheppard describes himself as a workaholic. The magazine *Business* observed: 'He never lets up and he does not know how to waste time', while Sheppard himself talked of his habit of going into a meeting with a 'very strong line' (which he expected others to challenge and, where appropriate, defeat). Common sense and hard work are his mainstays. 'Single mindedness is a strength in that it helps you to get on with things, but it doesn't make you particularly lovable or even balanced,' he says.

> Which brings us to the business of approbation. Those who seek approval probably have to learn not to. We leave doggedness and move to those 'c' words: commitment, confidence and courage.

Sometimes, as Greg Dyke points out, courage can come from the disinclination to let one's imagination wander. And from bloody-mindedness.

A friend of mine said I've been successful because I've absolutely no imagination at all and was never able to imagine failure. I never follow any rules – there's that Tom Peters line: you're going to get fired anyway, so break the rules. Nobody ever became successful in a company by following the rules, because they're devised by people above you who don't want to be successful.

That same bolshiness – the refusal to be bogged down by seeking endorsement from peers and associates – is seen in Anita Roddick. Here she is talking about what her husband perceives to be her winning attribute – and how she might use it:

> Gordon says it's my ability to cut through the crap and ask the question, which is often 'Why not?'
>
> We had an amazing new product, like a Play-Doh for kids, a soap that can be moulded and played with. But we had a packaging which was unacceptable in our company; it was like tin foil because you couldn't recycle – so it was out, no matter how innovative. Then we came up with a Bio-plastic product, a special plastic film which was recyclable. Only two weeks before manufacturing started, for whatever reason, the packaging couldn't be provided. Then I thought, no, I'll phone the bloody company myself and speak to the managing director. And we got it. Because I simply can't accept no for an answer.

Courage, though, is not recklessness – a distinction drawn by Peter de Savary, who once owned Aspinalls casino but who says that only fools gamble in business. There has to be a basis for expecting success:

> It's not a question of gambling. You don't gamble – you try to see an opportunity, see something where some added value, some change of circumstance that you can bring about – not market speculation at all, but somewhere where creativity, some degree of pioneering instinct, can change the nature of the adventure you've got yourself into and enhance its value.

To be successful, de Savary says, involves 'working hard, sticking to your guns and having the courage of your convictions'. But a pure entrepreneur needs the acceptance of losing money as 'part of the deal' – an inevitability that has to be managed and not allowed to abort the whole operation.

Lord Sheppard also credits himself with a lack of imagination: failure does not occur to him.

I do lack imagination, in the sense that it isn't that I set out to be a very courageous and bold – it's that personal survival never occurs to me. If you take the Pillsbury takeover, we realized we were betting ourselves, but as we weren't risking the shareholders, it didn't worry us. I don't mean we were stupid, but we never for one moment thought we would fail. We knew we were right strategically and, thank goodness, it proved to be right. Courage is vital, and lack of imagination helps with courage. I'm told many a VC [Victoria Cross] has got it because he didn't realize the bullets were intended for him!

In his book, *Maximum Leadership*, Sheppard uses passionate language about business: conviction, courage, inspiration, vision. He says:

I think you've got to believe. The danger is that people can fall in love with the business that they're in, and can get mesmerized by it, and as a result they don't actually see the business. Certainly I saw plenty of that in my 20 years in the motor industry. Having said that, you mustn't be blinded, but, on the other hand, you've got to feel quite passionately about it. All those words are a lot of what success is about. It is to do with a thing you don't often see in management text books – courage, and it's probably the thing you need most.

Few people have more experience of public acclaim and criticism than Jack Rowell. It is, he says, the heat of the kitchen he occupies, and while there are certain protective measures that can be taken – such as simply not reading bilious reports – it would be impossible to get through it without commitment:

Whatever I've done I've been very committed. I expect high standards of myself and also the other people involved. I wouldn't put up with people who didn't aspire to such standards. Great desire is important because life isn't straightforward all the time. That desire carries you through the issues when the pressure builds up. I say to myself, 'Do you want this? Then get on with it and forget the struggles you have to cope with at the moment.' It's heat from the kitchen – if you don't like it, get out.

Sports writer Steve Bale, grappling with the Rowell enigma in the *Sunday Telegraph*, talks of Rowell's 'tactical nous and iron resolve'. He is, Bale says, an outstanding motivator, showering his players with praise or rebukes irrespective of whether they were internationals or newcomers. In return, Bale says, his players displayed 'an almost divine will to win, the desire to be first'.

> Even so, there will be times when bad decisions or failures are inevitable. It is vital to take the right attitude.

Rick Parry is ruthless about regrets. He acknowledges his mistakes then puts them behind him. 'Never look backwards. That's not to say we didn't make mistakes, or to say we shouldn't have done things differently, but there is no point in having regrets.' He is not alone in this philosophy. Peter de Savary advocates shaking yourself down and starting again, going forward with eyes to the front, and keeping the damaging feeling of defeat at bay.

Defeat and disapproval, as Barry Hearn says, have to be kept in perspective. Walking on eggs will smash the eggs, that's all. In the Robert Half interview, he summed it up: 'The great thing about enjoying yourself and why I enjoy this sort of thing, frankly, is because you can be totally honest. It doesn't really matter. It doesn't matter if I upset you or vice versa, does it – we're unlikely to see each other again anyway...'

Mistakes, says Hearn, are part of the plot: 'The ability to make mistakes and to learn from them is essential. As Aneurin Bevan said, if I haven't made seven mistakes by lunchtime, I'm still in bed. The day anyone tells you they don't make mistakes, you're dealing with a complete prat. If you take decisions, you must make mistakes.'

> Success is rarely achieved alone. The ability to build a team is vital, and does not stop in the work-place.

Ron Dennis says he relies on the support of his wife as well as those he has around him:

The support of my wife is quite important. I am pretty damned difficult to live with. I am a perfectionist – everything in its place, which isn't easy when you've got three young children. I work very long hours and I'm not particularly disciplined in advising her when my hours are changing. That's a big plus. Then I've got some really good people around now who I've brought into the company and put through the process of 'McLarenizing', and they're very good.

Peter de Savary has his own philosophy about building his team. His PA has been with him for over a decade, and in his rather sparse London premises – where he sits in the general office – he is surrounded by people who have been with him for years:

> Perhaps the most important thing is, always be kind to people. Be kind to the person who's sweeping the corridor, be kind to the person who has to clean the loo, be kind to the person who's your right hand and a senior person, and try to be generous and fair. Try to treat them as an equal human beings even though their particular position in life at that moment is not the same as yours.

Sir Terence Conran also talks of the importance of team-building: 'I think you've got to be a very good team-builder and enthuser, because you have to have around you people who are probably not going to be paid very much, but must believe in you and your ideas and believe that they will eventually get good rewards.'

Prue Leith says it is vital, once having selected the team, to let them get on with their jobs.

> I actually think that a managing director's or chairman's job is to be a kind of sounding board for ideas. I don't think my job is to interfere with my divisional directors that they have to do this, do that, do it fast or do it tomorrow. I think my job is for them to come along and say they've had an idea, or why don't we do this, and then we'll talk it though. I feel my job is a kind of nanny – the job of a boss is to help people do what they do best. I employ cooks who cook much better than me, managers who manage much better than me, accountants who add up much better than me. My job is to help them to do their job terribly well, and then I get all the glory and they get all the work – and that seems like a very good division of labour!

But the team-builder par excellence – if not by any conventional means – is Jack Rowell, whose entire success on the rugby field, perhaps more than in his business career, depends on recruiting the right people. Rowell learned this, he says, at school:

I was captaining teams all the way through my schooling. When I look back I learned a lot without realizing it from that, and that's helped me in business. I learnt more about managing people when I was captain of the rugby team of Gosforth in the North East than when I was working for Proctor & Gamble, because you didn't pay them – they had to respect your leadership, otherwise you were in a fix. It's very similar.

Part of choosing the right team is selecting the right captain, as Rowell explains:

An England captain is under pressure to succeed and do well personally within that. He's got to have qualities that would clearly suit him for management in industry. By definition he's going to need to be a leader. Certainly he'll need to be a very good player so he's in the team. Someone who can keep a clear head because within the hurly-burly of the game of rugby in particular, the captain's got to be one step removed mentally and, despite the pressure, be able to organize what's happening on the field if it's not going the way one expected to start with. He's got to set a good example on and off the field behaviourally – integrity, courage for sure, and very importantly, competence in being able to fulfil the playing role.

> Then there is a matter of operating style – a conscious decision to do things in a certain way.

Lord Sheppard says cheating is off his agenda. 'I would never knowingly cheat, not because I would go to prison or be punished, but because it would just unhook everything I had done in my life. If I could win by cheating, what the bloody hell did I do all that work for?'

Chris Wright – in common with Rick Parry – cultivated the ability to listen properly, aligned with a sound grasp of his business and an awareness that he had to *offer*, not merely to respond:

I was a good listener. And you have got to sell yourself. Life is about selling, business is about selling, and you have to sell yourself in that situation. Then you have to know what you're talking about, so when he says he wants this kind of group and this is his budget, you can say 'I have this, this, this and this and by the way, there's another one I've heard of' – and of course, being able to deliver.

Parry settled on a principle for working as soon as he took on the task of putting together the Premier League:

Particularly in the early days, I genuinely believed every day was going to be my last, and through that I decided very early on that there was only one way to run things – always try to do what I genuinely believed was right for the League as a whole. There was always a temptation to try to spend your time pleasing each of the chairmen. That would definitely be the way to an early grave. If you focus on just doing your best, doing what's honest and doing what's right, you hope that at any point in time, more of the chairmen will be happy with what's happening than won't. There will always be someone complaining and some of them individually are always complaining whatever happens. There will always be someone unhappy, but you hope the majority are happy.

Parry says the essential ingredient in his success has been the refusal to deviate from this: 'Being prepared to listen and assimilate information. I'll be criticized for anything, but not for losing my integrity.'

There comes a stage in considering the essence of these people, however, when, it has to be faced that they may have strengths and attributes which came with their layette. They don't talk about these themselves, but others do. Some are born great, some achieve greatness and some have greatness thrust upon them, to paraphrase Shakespeare – but the power of mesmerism is probably something you have, or something you just wish you had.

Peter de Savary attracts adjectives and epithets as naturally as he breathes. One of his close business associates, Kit Hobday, described him thus: 'His two great assets are that he has the most superb line of chat of anyone I've ever met, and an ability to learn quickly. If he went into forestry, he would be an expert in 24 hours.'

Amanda Mitchison, writing for the *Independent* in 1994, visited de Savary at Skibo Castle and asked Hamish Thomson, de

Savary's contractor at Skibo (and a relative by marriage) if he was always so energetic. Thomson replied that he never stood still. Sarah Giddings, writing in the *Mail on Sunday* a year later, concluded that the secret of his appeal is actually quite simple. Peter de Savary is an enthusiast with an irrepressible energy and charm which his reputation belies. Mitchison concurred: 'It is surely the tycoon's persuasiveness, the mind-fuddling quantity of different projects he controls, this ability to conjure up loans from the Bahamas, that marks him apart. If Skibo were to flop, one feels he would merely move on. Multi-faceted and helium filled, de Savary would just bob back up to the surface somewhere else.'

In the *Sunday Telegraph*, Andrew Duncan wrote in 1985: 'It seems difficult to pin down exactly what he does... At Charterhouse, his academic ability soon became less conspicuous than the charm which has since clearly been a considerable element in his success.' An article in the *Sunday Times* nearly a decade ago quoted a former associate: 'He's got a hell of a personality and loads of charisma, he thrives on animal instinct and has a mind like a computer.' And to boot, he is also said to be 'mesmerizing'.

Jack Rowell, in his own words, is 'driven'. An analyst confirmed it for him, also offering the observation that he would 'go one day suddenly'! Rowell says:

I'm a driven person; if I'm not fully occupied I'm dangerous. When I've gone in on the odd occasion they used to put a gin and tonic in my hands straight away and then another one, and I'd say, 'What's this for? And they said they all know that unless you have some alcohol you'll be a very tense and touchy person, so we're trying to knock it out of you. So I think it's in me. I did the business and I did the sport – which I thought was an outlet, of course it was a different kind of challenge – but then I found that I was actually hyperactive, and that's me. If it's a gift, if you're gifted that way, so be it. I don't think of it as a vice.

Kate Battersby, writing in the *Sunday Telegraph* in 1995, said Rowell's coaching style was 'inspirational' rather than tactical, and he was frequently called Machiavellian (and sometimes a bully). In the *Daily Telegraph* the same year, writer John Mason said the tales about Rowell were legendary and quoted Stuart Barnes, outside-half-turned-journalist and Rowell's confidant in the transformation of

Bath. 'I sometimes think that while loyalty is important, in Jack's mind 100 per cent effort is better still,' Barnes said. 'He's got no time for excuses. He picks you for a job and expects you do it. If the opposition does it better, he won't tear out what hair he's got left, just as long as you've given it everything you've got and a bit more.'

Prue Leith says she is bossy, attention loving and vain: 'I think most restaurateurs are restaurateurs because they couldn't work for a big company like Trust House Forte – they do it because they are egotists. I like the attention. I am the only person I know who likes having my photograph taken. I hate seeing it, because I'm so vain I don't like the result, but I really like the attention!' But she also credits herself with enthusiasm. 'I hate the laid back,' she says.

Sir Terence Conran is 'known for thumping the table' but dislikes the idea that he is overbearing. 'I have to believe it, but I don't think I am. I want to encourage other people to come bubbling to the surface,' he told Charles Nevin, interviewing him for the *Independent on Sunday* in 1992. A friend described him to Nevin as a 'charismatic bully, intensely competitive, the type of person other people are desperate to make love them, because they hate the idea that he will not find them fascinating'.

Lord Sheppard is famous for a management style which he describes as 'a loose grip around the throat', but his successor at GrandMet, Sir George Bull, says of him: 'Allen does live up to his corporate myth, but I think that the man underneath is actually a bigger and more sensitive man than the cover story gives credit for.'

As well as qualities, an entrepreneur may have exceptional judgement – call it instinct or call it perception. *Business Age* wrote of David Lloyd: 'Marketing is his strong point, as potential members soon realize. Every trick in the marketing handbook has been used to increase revenues, plus a few never thought of before. Memberships in a David Lloyd club are almost always sold out before the club is built, such is the demand he creates.'

Conran has ridden the crest of public desire. He has given them shops they want, restaurants they want. He is a master of anticipation or, as he describes it, understanding what people might want before it is offered to them. 'Understanding people, understanding their aspirations and providing the goods, the service, the environment that gives them that surprise, that says, "Oh, that's something

I really like. I knew I really wanted it and here it is." That is the single thing,' he says. Then there is his formula, as demonstrated by Quaglino's restaurant in St James's. 'I knew that there would be a surprise of space as you came into a relatively modest entrance, and down some relatively modest stairs on to a platform, and then were able to look at this huge area with a lot of people in it (I hoped). It is a theatrical experience. That's what I say about restaurants – the back part is manufacturing, the front part is the retailing, the theatre is what holds the whole thing together.'

Quaglino's demonstrates his foresight as well as his design skills. He was constantly challenged about this large, noisy, 'democratic' vision that he had seen work in Paris.

> I was told that if London wanted a huge, busy, democratic restaurant, it would already have one. I said, 'What? London doesn't want this because it doesn't have one?' The idea that Parisians were very happy indeed with their La Coupôles and big brasseries but that they were totally different seemed to me to be ridiculous.
>
> It reminded me of the Habitat experience again; that Gatling gun approach to retailing; a lack of confidence; people making decisions on what they sold last year.

Conran's success as a restaurateur, he says, rests on his recognition that food is the most important factor, design and service come afterwards, and the result should be total enjoyment. 'I cannot divide food and design. Food and drink are the most important things but being a designer, I'm interested in the two aspects of design that concern a restaurant: the logistics so that it works properly, and the aesthetics, and the atmosphere that these create.'

Barry Hearn relies heavily on instinct. 'When Steve Davis walks into a room you're in the presence of something special. When Eubank walks into the room you have the same feeling. I can't really describe it. I had it when Sebastian Coe walked into the room and you get it to an extent with Linford Christie. When Rupert Murdoch walks into the room you feel like standing up. Eubank walked into the room, just in a tracksuit, and said, "I'm a sportsman" and we did a deal.'

Hearn opened up the advertising market for his stable of sporting celebrities. He says he works on his ability to understand and exploit other people's weaknesses:

When you're talking about selling, there's 100 different techniques for selling yourself or selling a product. There's a whole different ambit. The Italians have a word, *simpatico* – you have to be *simpatico*. You also have to have a little bit of steel in there because the real art, as Donald Trump will tell you, is once you've done all these little bits, the real art is closing. The other bit is easy, that's entertainment.

Andrew Davison, interviewing Hearn on a routine day in 1991, watched him change, chameleon-like, according to who he was dealing with. 'It is an extraordinary show underscored by a matey jocularity, often disguising its very real sense of purpose. But as those who have dealt with Hearn know: you underestimate him at your peril. He is a master of persuasion,' Davidson wrote.

And there is one last charm essential to success: good luck. As David Lloyd says: 'You need a lot of luck. I don't care what you do, but you need luck along the way. You make a lot of your own, but you still have to have it – it's got to break for you.' Rick Parry says luck has played a big part in his achievements; and if Mother Luck, as Barry Hearn calls it, were a snooker player, he'd have signed her up:

With all the brains in the world and all the opportunities and all the money, if you ain't got Mother Luck, you're still out there on the street. I've been fortunate and I've taken advantage. I've been tough when I've had to be, but I think most of all I've kept a sense of humour. I've had moments when I'm sitting in a place – Miami, Boxing Day – and my chief accountant rings me up and things are going bad, you know, losing money. And the boxing's slow and you think to yourself, 'Well, here we go.' And the accountant says a big double glazing company has just gone into liquidation and they owe us £750,000. My sense of humour just comes through at that moment. I look at my wife and say they've gone skint for 750 grand. She says, 'What did you say?' I say, 'Well, bollocks.' That's the only word that came to mind. You have to go through things and take into account that we're all lucky, we're all breathing. I know it's a naff thing to say but there's always someone worse off than you. When you look at us we're in the lap of luxury and you've just got to appreciate it. If you appreciate it no matter what, I wouldn't give anyone the pleasure of spoiling my day. That's what you need to have.

8 ENCOUNTERS WITH THE CITY

Pleasure or Pain?

I think if the opportunity came there are one or two people in the City who I would... well, let me put it like this: if one of them went under a bus tomorrow, I would hardly go to the funeral.

Greg Dyke, TV executive.

Ah, the City. Great buildings. Great bonuses. Great suits. Rubbing shoulders with the best that Savile Row can hand-stitch is surely a milestone in any professional career. Or maybe not. Once an entrepreneur tangles with the City – the merchant bankers, the analysts, the banks – he or she may find a figurative shark pool with operators as ruthless as the real thing. Turgid, unimaginative, totally disloyal, unfit to father babies (cf Anita Roddick), fickle... does no one have a good word for the money men? But ours is not to mitigate. The City is a tough old place, and the Adventure Capitalists do not find it a measure of success which brings them a great deal of pleasure.

One of the people least likely to be found on the grey streets of EC1 with a smile on her face is Anita Roddick. For 16 years until the early Nineties, The Body Shop and the City had a love affair. Then there was a profit set-back and the company was booted out of bed. Then there was a 33 per cent increase, and once again, the City was round on the doorstep with the roses and champagne. Roddick views all this with disdain. In fact, she thinks it's about time the City conducted a critical look at itself instead of turning its scrutiny on business with such rigour. It needs, she says, an audit of its values. It should look beyond the bottom line:

They are a turgid lot. Any institution at the end of a century, and now, at the end of a millennium, has to be the subject of change, whether it's a financial institution or political or academic institution. What is so sad about the City is that it has no real reverence for any business being seen as either community or shared common interest or incubators for the human spirit, or just new playgrounds of creativity. I don't think they even like profits: they love the difference between one six-month set of profits and the other, and the notion of measuring a company by what they call its bottom line. My argument is: keep the bloody bottom line at the bottom, that's where it should be. Bring in the values, bring in the ingenuity of business, its creativity, its product, its culture, its myths – that's the stuff of business.

The culture of The Body Shop is that it's hard to measure on any of the economic indicators. How do you measure education? How do you measure joy in the work-place? How do you measure people's happiness or the aesthetics of a work-place? A corporation should be measured too by how it screws up the environment or what it gives to the planet, or indeed by social audit. Business doesn't come with moral compassion. No matter how you may argue, the large transnationals aren't there for the pursuit of human spirit. They are there for the profit, and more often than not, for the greed of individuals rather than public good.

Roddick is successful enough to have no truck with the City and The Body Shop's approach to corporate mores (as opposed to ethical mores) has been described as 'cavalier'. Roddick puts it more colourfully:

Let me tell you, you wouldn't marry them or have their babies. They have no concept. They're trading in the faeces of a company. When they come, they don't ask about the products or the innovation or the idea. They ask dumb questions like, 'What's the gearing?' Give me a break! Is this the stuff of innovation? I think in my company, they trawl me out, when the City come down to see us, just to give them shock therapy.

If or when Roddick begins an alliance against the City, she may be able to count on the support of Greg Dyke. Dyke turned London Weekend from a £70 million company to a £750 million company in four years, and shares bought at 70p were worth £7. It didn't stop institutional shareholders accepting the Granada shilling:

I don't blame Granada; they played the game. They owe no loyalty to us, but if you multiplied somebody's money ten-fold in four years they owe you, and I think it tells you about the problems. The interesting thing about business is that almost everyone I know who works in the City thinks what they do has real value; they're important people and that it matters. And nearly everyone I know in business thinks the City is a bunch of prats who have no value to society at all. That's my conclusion. To go around in a hostile bid trying to persuade someone who has 1.5 per cent of us not to vote against you, when you're opposite someone whom you probably wouldn't give a job to, having to say 'please sir' is very unpleasant. Then you discover the reason they sold is that they haven't made their target that month! That's no way of funding a business.

Dyke left LWT – rich but angry – rather than work under his new masters. In an interview with the *Independent on Sunday* the same year, he said the turning point had been when Mercury Asset Management decided to sell. 'The fact that we had been one of their best-performing shares was irrelevant. Other companies in which they have shares should take note,' he said.

Dyke says he is still bitter about the institutions selling out. 'Did I feel bitter then? I feel bitter now. But now I put it on the back burner and can smile again. What do the Italians say about revenge? That it is a dish best served cold. I think if the opportunity came there are one or two people in the City who I would... well, if one of them went under a bus tomorrow, I would hardly go to the funeral.'

On the whole, he says, the City is interested only in the short term – 'We delivered for them... they are not to be trusted.'

What does Sir Terence Conran recall about the City? Spots, among other features. He noticed them on the faces of some of the ambitious young men to whom he had to speak nicely during the takeover bids for Storehouse. 'We had something like 18 months trying to defend our position, trudging round the institutions, seeing the same spotty youths again and again.' This ordeal ended with Conran backing out before schedule to reassess how he wanted to spend his life. Or, more exactly, how he didn't want to spend it.

He's not bitter, sitting just across the river in his office and contemplating the streets around which he found himself traipsing. The City, he says, 'gets its just deserts... I was a willing player in that particular game and I was trying to do things for the right reason,' he said in the *Sunday Telegraph*. 'The City was the way I could do it. Some things worked, some didn't.' Even so, 'spotty youths' are among those he would still rather avoid, along with financial journalists.

> I quite enjoyed that period of building, first going public with Habitat, then during my other corporate career. I don't regret it in any way; I learned a lot about the City, about short termism. Short termism is one of the ills of this country; you are always expected to produce instant results. However much you say it's going to take five years to change this company, and you can't do things overnight, always the analysts will believe that you're going to do it overnight. It's very bad for the country, certainly if you're in a capital-intensive business, such as manufacturing, which has declined so radically in this country – you have huge investment in plant and machinery and it won't give you an instant pay-off. The short-term attitude of our City is certainly not the same in Japan or Germany. In this country, companies are put under intense scrutiny and it is very demoralizing for management to get this constant criticism of their business by people who are less interested in long-term success than short-term profitability.
>
> This was a Thatcherism. She was convinced that this short-term attitude in the City was good for the business in the country. It could work... in war, there is always innovation, and she believed business would go better if it was under pressure. She could not see how important long-term capital investment was.

David Lloyd's relationship with those who control the strings of many and various purses changed dramatically as his clubs grew more successful. Before he built the first one, he needed large injections of money, but persuading anyone to lend it to him was a challenge:

> Banks throw money at you when you're doing well, but actually to get started is a very difficult thing. Some of the meetings I went to, it was just a head-butt job, to be quite honest – you would go in trying to sell a concept that nobody had ever seen. Therefore I couldn't prove it and said that there wasn't such a thing – that was why I wanted to do it – and it went on and on and on.
>
> One meeting I went to, they said they wanted to lend me money and become a shareholder. I went and sat in an office and the directors came

in, and we sat at a lovely table with a chap serving us with lovely long white gloves – silver platter with a pot of tea – and one chap asked me what I wanted to do. I said I wanted to build a tennis centre, and he asked where was the nearest bus stop. I asked him whether he played golf and how he got to the golf club. He said 'By car,' and I said that was how you were going to get to my club. As it happens, there was a bus stop outside, but that wasn't the point. Then he said to me, or someone else said to me, 'What's it worth for a warehouse?'

To cut a long story short, I picked the stuff up and disappeared. I must have had hundreds of meetings where you just thought in the end, 'What am I doing? How can I get this thing started?, In the end, I had Midland Ventures wanting to put some money in, and Barrett builders. That's how it started. At the end of the day I had two battling for the same piece of the action, so obviously I got a good deal. Midland Ventures were a very good venture capitalist company to get involved with, because most venture capitalists want their money out after two or three years. They want their 42 per cent return – mega-return – and are not really interested. You're just a number on the wall and that's it. That wasn't the case with Midland Ventures – the guy took an enormous interest. [The guy – Ian Taylor – was later offered the job of Lloyd's managing director.]

For Lloyd, flotation (in 1993) was good. It raised the profile as well as raising money, and brought in offers of sites. It was also good for staff morale:

> Midland and myself agreed that shares at the same price should be offered to the staff and a lot of them took them up, so we built up quite a large shareholding and then introduced share option schemes. We must have more than 60 or 70 of the staff who have been with me from the beginning and they've all got share options. They're important, and they really do value it. I'll be driving home in the car and I'll get a phone call – 'What happened, they went down 3p!'

But even Lloyd, with his comparatively benign view, can see clear drawbacks with the City's short-term view, which were inflexible towards businesses with an idiosyncratic growth pattern. He found himself under pressure to develop two new clubs a year, which he had said he aimed to do, to keep up with the City's preferred rate of expansion. The City was more concerned to see this target met than to be sure the right site had been picked after careful and thorough consideration:

> You get this terrible gearing. Gearing in our business is very short term, like project finance. Everybody is looking at this figure, and you can't go the odd 50 per cent or 75 per cent. Why that is set in stone from an analyst's point of view I'm not really sure, because it's not how high it goes, it's how quickly it comes down that counts. You can bring it down very quickly in our business. A tennis centre costs £6 million and from day one we actually operate at a profit and the gearing goes down dramatically. We have to try to convince people that this magic figure is for us, what we believe is a very liveable situation for the short term, because we have to expand. We don't want to slow our growth down; we want to take this company bigger and bigger, under control. There is an enormous market out there. Glasgow was our fastest-growing membership, except Finchley, which was full by the first day. If it works in Glasgow it must work in Edinburgh. We have about 700 indoor courts – Holland has 3,000. Then there were the analysts...
>
> Some of the analysts write a report without seeing the business. For them to do this just by picking up the phone and asking a few questions without seeing what happens is bad. I think they have to come down and view it and ask questions there, and ask members. Three or four analysts are perhaps too busy – but then they shouldn't write you up. They are putting that circular out to people who buy shares or not, as the case may be. It's not their money these guys are spending.

Lord Sheppard found himself under heavy questioning by the City during the 'brain surgery' he and his colleagues carried out at GrandMet, shedding the hotels which had been the start of the company. When he retired, the share price was lower than it had been at its peak. But he did not blame the City – if GrandMet's strategy had not been appreciated by the City, he said, it was probably due to 'bad communication and bad salesmanship':

> We were building a long-term strategy and they were interested in the immediate. Why not sell and come back later as an investor? Against this understandable positioning we found it impossible to convince investors to give us short-term support, however much our long-term strategy was right.
>
> We'd moved at great speed on reshaping the business. We reshaped the portfolio and got down from 28 business sectors to two, food and drink. On the remaining businesses, we then went through a re-engi-

neering process and came up with £500 million worth of restructuring provisions. If you looked at these as an investor, they yielded a payback of about 18 months. Not bad, but disturbing for short-term investors.

But of course, just to add insult to injury to those investors in doubt, we then recycled all those savings back into marketing because we were trying not to put up the next year's profits but build brands for the future. None of those were very popular things to do, and one can understand that. It was pretty damned hard work for everybody and in that process, you frighten some people to death!

For Peter Savary, the City's desire for steady and reliable growth is anathema and, he says, a rein on entrepreneurism:

The pressure from the City is more on public companies and the public sector. That's one of the reasons why many entrepreneurs – I think unfortunately – are not in the public sector. It's very hard for an entrepreneur to accurately predict that every six months the profits are going up, the net worth value of the shares is going up, and to maintain it in a consistent graph.

The City is very fickle. They're absolutely gung-ho with you one one day and they're not very tolerant when it isn't going to plan. It is extremely difficult to maintain continual growth in all sectors on an even curve. You'll have some of this if you're an entrepreneur – a bit of that, and a whole lot of that. It's a bit of a roller-coaster, and you have to have the stomach and the appetite for it, and you take the risk and you only gamble a little bit on that particular venture. And you can afford to lose it, God forbid, or take a loss on it, but quite often you get a very good healthy return on it. So it's part of a balanced portfolio. I think it's very difficult for really entrepreneurial people to be under that scrutiny and the demands of the City [with its] 'Well, what do you mean the last six months we've gone down 10 per cent, I mean what the hell's going to happen in the next six months?' And then, whatever you say, you're hanged by it.

Will this always be the case? Anita Roddick says it need not be:

Financial institutions are human institutions, designed by people and capable of being redesigned. Business is creative and short-term profits will be seen to be one of the most rapid ways of devaluing, or indeed destroying, our planet. There has to be a shift in consciousness. Poverty is often caused by big business interests; it has to be responsible; it has to come with moral compassion. What business can do in the future is take that notion of responsibility, not only for its shareholders but for the bigger agenda of the community, of the planet itself. I know this may sound airy-fairy but it is an absolute firm belief in our company. We listened 15 years ago to the environmental movement, who were considered flakies then. Nobody was listening to them. We took note and as a result we are conducting our company according to that information. We bring in new economic thinkers, telling us the real problem with scenarios that leave me absolutely afraid. There is so much information about the diminution of resources. Business has to have a global perspective and understand global issues, and I hope The Body Shop will continue to challenge that. I'm not going to be part of any company that diminishes either our values, our personal creed of behaviour or the planet. I'd rather leave.

> So the City is a spoiler for some, much less one of the spoils. What then, are more valid measurements of success?

Anita Roddick: 'Success is something I haven't thought about. I feel successful because the alternative New Academy business school, that I talked about, happened. Or all our staff being human-rights literate and our shops used as safe havens for collecting data on human rights abuses – when that happens it will be something else. If I see myself as successful, which is never going to be on financial terms, because that's not a measurement, it will have to be on a human value scale. But if you say you're successful it means there's not change. You know there's no more.'

Barry Hearn: 'Success gives me the opportunity and the platform to live out a little bit more of the fantasy that I'm living out at the moment. In a way, I am [motivated by money]. I don't win cups and belts and trophies. I can only actually judge success... when I was losing a million pounds a year or whatever, that looked like I was a failure. So my motivation is to be successful but, having got there, then I don't really know what to do with it from here.'

Lord Sheppard: 'A journalist quoted John Prescott as saying "We're all middle class now" and asked how I felt about that statement. I said I didn't know, because I regard myself as successful working class. You asked me what my 91-year-old mother, who is still alive, thinks of it. She's quietly proud and gets a bit upset when she sees me being attacked in the papers, so we've stopped telling her. Her eyes aren't good and she can't read it so we just tell her the good bits. It's been quite amazing. I've been very lucky because of my parents and my wife.'

Jack Rowell: 'I get a lot of personal satisfaction out of my team winning and the individuals doing well. That gives me a big kick. Over many years at Bath, when we were winning things, I wouldn't feature at all in anything. It happens nowadays, you don't pursue the publicity of it. The best thing I would do, later on, is get my car and play my CD player, play my music to myself and go for a drive, and just feel good about life.'

Peter de Savary: 'I measure success by finally reaching the point where you have defined what you believe is the specific opportunity... and you have a vision which is, God, I can see the whole thing finished, I can see it as it should be. Then you work out how much money it's going to take, where you're going to get the money from, how you're going to structure it, is it viable? You do the business plan and all the other things... then you not only have the vision but are completely convinced of its reality. And that, for me, is the measure of success. Do we achieve or do we fail? And quite honestly, whether that makes £50,000 or £5 million, for me, is of no consequence because I never go into things because they make more money than this one here. I go into things because they are going to be profitable, I think the returns are going to be attractive, I think the risk rewards are acceptable to me. I can't wait to get started because it's so exciting and so exhilarating and I can't wait to get it finished.'

Prue Leith: 'I suppose because I'm an egotist, I really do enjoy the fact that I have been successful. I like to be proud of things. Nothing upsets me more than if we screw up – I mean, I don't sleep, even over little things. If we've got something wrong it really upsets me.'

Sir Terence Conran: '[I measure success] by the pleasure I get out of the business. By going into The Conran Shop when it is absolutely bustling and full with people on a Saturday, going into a restaurant, going into Quaglino's or one of the others when there is a real hum, today gives me far more pleasure than the profits. I would not like to run an unsuccessful business, because that's why we are in business, not to make a loss. But people enjoying what has been offered to them is the thing that gives me real satisfaction.'

9 GOLDEN RULES
Rules of thumb, axioms and other insights

Dreams are important to have but you mustn't get carried away with the concept. If the numbers don't stack up... you can't make it work. It's pure numbers.
David Lloyd, tennis player and founder of David Lloyd fitness centres.

'Individualism is marvellous, but he who squeezes all the juice out of the lemon without leaving any for the next man is asking for trouble.' This wisdom (and wit) from Peter de Savary fails to feature so far in any book of quotations, but it is not hard to see its usefulness to a deal-maker.

Not everyone, of course, does deals. Some people are content to administer for a living. Rick Parry, indeed, has administered with such diligence and excellence that thousands of men (and women, maybe) would give their eye teeth to change their office seat for Rick's swivel chair at Liverpool Football Club, with 'chief executive' on the nameplate on the door.

Our subjects lack common aims or objectives, but share many traits, plus a wealth of experience in the cardinal sins of business, and the attitudes, approaches and devices they have found essential. Plus the odd trick or two.

One of the fascinating discoveries of this exploration of successful people has been how much they have learned to trust their gut instincts. We shall explore this further in the next chapter, when we look at how this has translated into their recruitment and management techniques. In this chapter, we will take a broader view, moving from Rick Parry's cool-headed negotiating skills to Ron

Dennis's view on the personal requirements of a Formula One racing driver.

Rick Parry is perhaps the medium through which most of us could recognize our personal potential. An accountant who knew he wanted to work in sport, he is an example of how skills can be built up and moved. He has exposed himself to a variety of experiences – including advising Manchester on its Olympic bid – and has learned how to marshal the breadth of his expertise. Many of us fail to appreciate the extent of our own knowledge.

Here is Parry talking about the problems of trying to put together the Premier League, negotiating on TV rights to its games and, subsequently, being offered the job of chief executive at Liverpool:

> On the one hand I was trying to do the negotiation on behalf of the clubs and on the other hand I was trying to keep half the clubs who wanted to be involved away from it. There were all sorts of interesting pressures, but through my previous existence with the Olympic bid I'd actually learned a fair bit about the relationship of sport and television and the valuations of rights, albeit then on a theoretical basis, so it was quite nice being able to put it into practice...
>
> Like in any negotiation, the reality was that it was all about competition, and the secret was just trying to keep the bidders in the ring. This isn't the easiest thing, because they don't like losing, and if one of them thinks they're not seriously in the running they'll withdraw, at which point the other one's bid will collapse too. So keeping them at each other's throats until the last minute was something of challenge. We had an idea of the sort of model we were looking for – that was important – but it's not what we finally ended up with because we had to match our aspirations with those of the TV companies. If Sky hadn't had the BBC alongside they wouldn't have got that deal; that terrestrial component was absolutely vital.

In negotiation, Parry says, it is a mistake to go for broke:

> This is not a traditional football view, that you should always leave something on the table. At the end of the day if you're creating a partnership, you have to leave something there for your partner. If you screw the very last penny, that doesn't bode well for the longer term. What we wanted Sky to do was invest in promoting the game, in technology, new coverage techniques, which they did supremely well. We

wanted it to be a great partnership from their point of view, simply because we needed football to be the absolute must-have product for them when it came round to bidding again. We had to be in a position where the Premier League was such good news for Sky that they couldn't afford to lose it. If we'd sort of raped them the first time round and the thing hadn't worked for Sky we'd have been left high and dry the second time round.

When offered the Liverpool job, however, Parry's heart took over. He had to have it. 'That was the perfect job for me. It was a real no-brainer and took no decision time at all. It was my club from birth and having done two TV deals at the Premier League, I was starting to feel that maybe the time was right to move on. I wouldn't have missed it for the world – it was great fun, but a fairly life-shortening career, working for 20 chairmen, never something I envisaged doing for ever. So it was perfect timing in a way. I wanted to stay in football without doubt.'

The rules of the Parry league are these: move your skills around and don't think you're restricted to one discipline; have a goal in mind and be prepared to modify it; don't screw your partners; and if you get the chance of your dream job, grab it.

Chris Wright, a strong believer in instinct, says he has never had a master plan:

The important thing is to seize opportunities (and know one when you see one). The key thing to developing a business from scratch is that you have to be adept and be able to see opportunities rather than be stuck to a plan that tells you where you want to be in a few years' time. The plan is good, but not if it excludes the opportunity to be able to take those chances as they crop up.

Lord Sheppard would concur. But, he says, while the heart has to win in the end, it should only be after a rational analysis. He is quoted on the same topic in the book *Roads to the Top*: 'In taking a career decision, it is important to understand clearly what one is doing and why; to have thought it through, not to knee jerk. Choose positively to join the new company, rather than move only in order to leave the other company.' He learnt this when he failed to heed his own advice: 'I left Ford for negative reasons. It was a desperately tight decision and could easily have gone the other way, because I did amazingly well at Ford. Ultimately, you look rationally at the costs and benefits and then you must let your heart win.'

David Lloyd is not a believer in letting the heart rule. First, he says, you need to have something staked in your venture (in his case, it was his savings and his house – it need not be quite so drastic, but there has to be some investment that would cause some pain if it were lost). Then, if these are lacking, you have to learn patience and cultivate persistence: 'Every night I would come home and think what the hell am I doing this for? Then I would look back to Canada and think, "Well, it's done there, and it works" and you just keeping going on – and eventually it clicks.'

Keeping sight of realism, however unpalatable it appears, cannot be abandoned. If it is a venture that requires a big investment, there comes a time when the sums have to be examined with detachment. David Lloyd again:

> A lot of people are very optimistic. When I see financial studies on tennis centres they're very optimistic – actually, you have to be pessimistic on the number of people that are going to go in, and high on your costs. If it works then, you know it's going to work. If it doesn't you walk away from the deal. If it doesn't stack up and you don't get your return you walk out the door – it's as simple as that. You can't make it work, and you can't manipulate the figures. We did our figures on 70 per cent occupancy, on what we felt was a low fee. It took off immediately and we got 100 per cent in numbers, so it worked. Everyone should be very cautious. Dreams are important to have but you mustn't get carried away with the concept. It's pure numbers.

And if the venture cannot move – and a purpose-built tennis centre is not easily referred to Pickfords – location is everything:

> Location is a thing I learnt from Barretts. Location, location, location is the thing with any retail or leisure business. If you're in the wrong place, it doesn't matter who you've got managing it, it isn't going to work. It's much better having a great location and bad management team because you can change the management, but you can't change the location. You're there forever.

Lloyd's dispassionate nature is demonstrated by his retrospective view of his career actually playing tennis (rather than facilitating other people's playing). Or maybe not... beneath the suit, beneath the business persona, there is the soft underbelly of a man who would have chosen sporting greatness. Rather than excelling in business, he would have triumphed at Wimbledon:

> I would have wanted to win Wimbledon, but I wasn't good enough. All I can say is that I gave 100 per cent and I think I got the most out of my ability. That's another thing I tell every young kid that comes through the [tennis] scheme – you will succeed if you get to the top of your ability. If that's 150th, you've succeeded. When you have a given talent you have to make it work for you and if you don't, then you actually have failed – you've got something special, but you haven't worked hard enough.

Simplicity is Prue Leith's byword. Radish roses are not among her favourite things:

> It means being simple with our suppliers. We try to treat our suppliers exactly as we treat our customers. And simplicity with our customers, they get what they expect to get. If we do a trial meal for them we make every effort we possibly can so that the food they get on the night of the big banquet for 400 is exactly the same food as it would have been for four people. It's not a mission statement, but it does help us to run the company in a very focused way. I'm very against jargon. I just like good food a and the easiest way to do it is to make people proud of what they do.

Simplicity, says Leith, is 'deep in our philosophy':

> I can get very pompous about this. I'm against words like 'mission statement' and 'vision' and 'empowerment' and 'benchmarking' because they're used to death and they sometimes don't mean a lot. We have this motto, 'Simply Better', and it really is embedded in the business. It comes up all the time and we stand up and account for it. If you have a motto like that, it does challenge your management to live up to it. The reason we chose Simply Better – and we took a long time – was that we tried to think, 'Well, what are we?' We are very simple cooks, we don't go in for radish roses and things, but we do believe in the best ingredients. We started with the food and we thought we were better than our

rivals, better than yesterday – continual improvement all the time, and better than expectations. The 'simply' side doesn't just mean simple food, it means simple relationships. Our staff should know what's expected of them and if it's not simple and clear, our manuals written in plain English and not jargon or garbage – which I can't bear – they can't use them.

Anita Roddick's maxim is to remain true to your values. She has become a role model for young people. How should this be handled? 'I take it as a responsibility. I try to instil the concept that you have to be an activist, that you can't just be passive citizens, and must stand up and be counted. The medium that we give our staff is the playground of the company.'

Work, she says, does not need to be done in an environment of dour, cheer-free application. On the contrary: people will respond to being treated properly.

There's this wonderful notion of creating entertainment in the workplace – having a sense of carnival atmosphere – so we have all these old-age pensioners and Women's Institutes and schoolkids that go round. They see our recycling and our water filtration plant, they see how we manufacture. All of these things are providing stories and the myths and legends of the company and all the staff are interactive with it. We house nearly 1,000 people in our headquarters. It's wonderful and it humanizes the place. I love the interaction with the people who come.

The Roddick values, she says, are:

Listening to the church and the temple, that's all they are. Being kind, being respectful, trust, honesty, not lying – giving a modicum of trust and freedom. With the franchisees, most of them are husband and wife teams or partners in environmental life or teaching, who want to make an honourable life, do something beyond just a pay packet.

Barry Hearn was impatient to do well but patience, he says, is a business virtue he has learned. From being a shover, he has become more of a nudger. This is what he says about his plans for Leyton Orient: 'I don't have a rush. I've always been a long-term player in all my sports and really allowed it to develop at its own speed and just nudged it along, and I'll do the same with football.'

Hearn has one underpinning philosophy that he remembers in negotiating on behalf of his stable of sportspeople. 'You've got to have sportsmen who want glory, and you need people like me to make sure that we, the people that enjoy their glory, pay the price they deserve for giving us a special moment in our lives.'

However, we have moved too far on in the Hearn operation. First, there is one important hurdle to get past – that businessman's gut feeling. Without that, Hearn says, there is no deal. In fact, even the first conversation is unlikely to materialize:

> I used to have a general rule that I don't do business with someone I don't like. Now I've changed that. If I don't like them, I say I'm awfully expensive. I learnt that from Deryck Healey when we sold a knitting contract. I was asked to value the contract and it came to 20,000 US dollars. Deryck said, 'But Barry, these people are disgusting, chasing after the girls in the office, they are really horrible. It's got to be $200,000. I have to add a nought on if I've got to tolerate these people.' And they signed for five years! Amazing! So I suppose we've all got our price, but a gut feel separates the men from the boys. Once you've made the commitment your head has to rule your heart from that stage, otherwise you go off in an uncontrolled fashion. I love it when I do things with my heart, but it always costs me money.

Giving advice is one thing; taking it another. Greg Dyke declares himself 'almost too pompous' to have a business philosophy, but believes in two maxims: don't make your staff feel irrelevant or uninvolved. 'I run people. My job is to motivate a bunch of people. I think the rule about not having more than four levels from top to bottom is interesting, and if you have more than that, break it up.'

Overlarge hierarchies are joined by supercilious management techniques on Dyke's list of business *bétes noires*:

> There has always been a problem about people who get promoted in certain areas thinking that their major job is to make sure people underneath them don't challenge them or threaten them, so they don't tell them anything. The more you can actually say that this is the problem, this is what we're trying to achieve, this is the target, this is the weekly report, the better.

In managing people, Dyke says, the best vehicle is the team:

That's what programme teams do; they're wonderful. You have a team of 30 people making a programme. Everybody cares, everybody goes to the programme meetings. It doesn't matter whether they're the junior secretary or the guy or woman running the whole thing. They all go; they all care; they all laugh together, and when it works, they're all motivated by it.

Ron Dennis was bad at taking advice because it sat uncomfortably with his character. Yet, in retrospect, if he could have heeded one rule, it would have been to do more thinking and less hasty acting. Dennis says:

If you could have got me to think more, and act less, I think I would have got to where I was going faster and taken better decisions along the way. It's also important to put yourself in the right environment to think. People don't think enough, they just let their mind work by taking things in and randomly processing them. That's not thinking. Thinking is an analytical process by means of which you've got to define in your own mind the goal and objective you are seeking. Then you've got to decide what the variables are and work out where they fit in, making something of a mental chess game. It's the carpenter's old value: think twice and cut once. Yet it is almost impossible to instil this into the minds of young people. They don't understand. Their minds and brains are still growing.

Many of us will at this point recognize that we don't have Ron Dennis's mental discipline and would struggle to gain it. So perhaps we could pursue a career on the circuit. Could driving a Grand Prix car really be an easier seat for us to occupy than safely negotiating the M25? Ron Dennis is quick to disabuse the reader of that notion.

It's different from driver to driver. They have to be very focused, they have to be disciplined, they have to be committed. They have to be tremendously fit, and by that I don't mean going through some trivial jogging process and eating the right things. We're talking Olympic standards here, based around a carefully constructed training programme which is rigorously adhered to.

The top drivers are incredibly hard on themselves and their ideal physique is not what an athlete normally needs. You don't need a lot of muscle because muscle takes oxygen and it is quite difficult to breathe deeply in a racing car. So you have to understand about developing the right muscles and understand all about hydration and the need to eat the correct foods to sustain your effort in the latter part of a race. If you understand this sufficiently, you can discern when a driver isn't in peak condition because his performance will drop off during the course of a race. This is never an issue with the really great drivers, because they understand and they get it done.

In addition, there are other levels of commitment that a driver needs to make in Formula One. The manner in which they conduct their private lives indicates how strongly they are going to perform in the long term. Interestingly, the really successful ones rarely get married before they've achieved some of that success. Marriage and commitment to a sport of this nature are extremely difficult to blend and the environment in which they operate is not particularly conducive to a worthwhile personal relationship. Don't get me wrong; these remarks shouldn't be construed as criticisms of marriage. Personally, I'm very much for it, but it is just something I observe in connection with the really great drivers across the years.

Sir Terence Conran's axioms are, like his design, uncluttered and essentially simple. This is not, however, to understate the difficulty of executing them, especially in creative fields. And some of them will translate into many business arenas. Here he is, on what he looks for when he recruits people – echoing a sentiment that is more relevant to commerce than it is perhaps given credit for:

First, people who I actually like. People I can have a conversation with, with a sense of humour, I think are honourable. Then you look at ability and their track record and you ask their friends about them. But most importantly of all, it is someone with whom you can have that essential dialogue, that you can sit down with a cup of coffee together and spend 15 to 20 minutes talking about a problem in a very loose, easy, friendly way and come to a decision. You only have one life and you have to enjoy it, especially for me because I don't see a division between work and leisure. Many people say that they can tolerate things at work because when they leave work, they leave it behind. I don't.

On the ingredients for a successful restaurant:

If you're not selling good food and not demonstrating good value for money, then it's not going to be a good restaurant. That is primarily why people go. But if that food is not supported by a good atmosphere, good design, good lighting, and excellent service, the restaurant is not going to have that essential atmosphere it needs to be successful. It is like retailing – the merchandise is the most important single thing, but the ambience of the store and the service are both very important components.

Conran has been a designer all his life, which gives him an advantage in the visual world. Watching his client base – literally and figuratively – has been his bedrock. The point he makes is that whatever the business, an operator must be acutely aware of the people he or she looks to for custom.

Practically everything I do is to do with visual matters. I look and observe all the time, what people are doing and what they are thinking about and what they are reading. I look at the newspapers they're reading, at the cafés they're visiting, at the magazines, at the TV, at the films they're watching to see the influences on them. Where they go on holiday... all these things get gathered and go into the computer and sorted and then you delve back into that when you have a problem to solve.

A sense of 'the moment' has been essential. It is not enough, either, to concentrate on domestic fashion and trends. For Quaglino's, he based the ambience on the large French brasserie, correctly anticipating that metropolitan Britain (especially London, with its cosmopolitanism and ease with European influences) was ready to move away from the invisible but omnipresent 'class divides' of its eating houses:

These very big restaurants have a different quality to them from those which you will find generally in London. They are entirely democratic places: there are all sorts of ages of people and all sorts of income groups can mix together, all sorts of socio-economic classes, and that to me gives something very interesting, a ménage of people. There was nowhere in London where you could do that.

Conran's grand rule for retailing – a tenet on which the early Habitat led the way and which has never really been bettered – is this: get a philosophy, and get your own brand. 'It seems to me very important indeed that a retailer should have a philosophy.' Conran says:

They should know what they are doing and be able to transmit to every-body in their company what their company stands for, what it believes, what it is going to do. I also believe very strongly that a retailer should be creating its own-brand merchandising. When you go into a Walt Disney store, for instance, you come out with Walt Disney merchandise. If you go into Sainsbury's, you come out with Sainsbury's merchandise.

I believe the great change which happened in merchandising was the retailers' own merchandise could not be sold by a Costco selling at a discount down the road... you cannot build a retail business when you are constantly being undermined by discount... Every retailer with muscle should build their own brand. You cannot discount on Gap products, can you? You cannot get your hands on them. Gap has an extremely good, strong identity and it has products stamped 'Gap'. You can control your own destiny when you have this brand, and play your margin games with your own products.

Finally, says Conran, there is an important matter of style. In commerce, indecision is a killer: 'Making no decision is the worst decision. Delaying a decision is a perfectly good decision to make, but if you let people know you are indecisive, you cannot lead your company.'

All these principles, and more, are corroborated by Peter de Savary. Few have more experience than him of highs and lows, boom and bust, of the magic of success and the dejection of failure. Entrepreneurism, he says, is based on understanding one basic fact: that it is a decision-making process like any other, but with different risks:

You have to, in life, make decisions all the time. Decisions when you grow up, decisions when you get married, decisions when you have children, decisions on how you're going to make a living, how you're going to meet your obligations, how you're going to improve your own family's and your friends' and your employees' quality of life. And there are many ways to do it. I've chosen to do it in what I would regard as an entrepreneurial manner, which is taking risks. I take those risks on a fairly regular basis. Some are large, some are small. But the essence of being an entrepreneur is to take a risk and try to evaluate the risk-reward ratios. And accept when you take that risk, having thought about it as best you can, done what you believe is right, to evaluate is it a good or bad decision, but having taken that decision to always recognize that you could be wrong.

As de Savary says, losing money is part of the deal for an entrepreneur, but gambling is a bad move: there has to be an identifiable opportunity to make a difference to the purchase and change its nature. If there is a deal – and de Savary is known for being a great deal-maker – there must also be two parties:

> When you talk about making a deal you imply that there have to be two parties. And the first thing I always consider is, is there actually a deal here? By that, I mean you have to be sure that there is a deal in it for the other side, be they the buyer or the seller or indeed, somebody coming into a joint venture or partnership. Because if there isn't a deal in it for them, or if you don't all believe there's a deal for both parties at the outset, it's quite likely that one or other party is going to be upset, disappointed, and feel badly or frustrated later on. So I always try to look at how this is going to work out for the other side as well as myself. Not today, when we do it, but as we go down the road. What are their anticipations? Is there something in it for both of us?

Screwing the other party to the boards, de Savary says, is never good policy. Or, as he puts it: 'Leave a squeeze in the lemon for the next man, don't try to squeeze it all. The friendship and relationship and goodwill that come from that can be very valuable in the future.'

A deal-maker also has to be able to think strategically: there may be another way. The first and obvious appeal of a venture may not be the one to go on. De Savary found this with Skibo Castle in the Highlands. Bought as a 'weekend cottage' during one of his business boom periods, he soon realized it was a mistake. But only as a weekend cottage. He looked at how to turn it round.

Once a business is established, a fast way to ruin is to take your eye off the ball. De Savary has another colourful parallel: a pilot does not perform a successful take-off then listen to music through his headphones for the rest of the trip. This rule is 'keep tabs on it':

> It's a question of how you treat the people that work with you: your suppliers, your customers; how you respond when things get tough, how you handle things going wrong. And trying at all times to look at your financial position in the business and on an almost daily basis – but if you don't do it weekly you're going to find it hard to maintain a business over many years – trying to look and say, what's going wrong,

what could go wrong, I've got this one big order and what happens if they don't pay me, what will it do to my cash flow, what happens if I don't get these potential orders?

You have to be like an airline pilot or any other aeroplane pilot. He's not supposed to sit there and listen to music on the headphones when he's flying across America. He's supposed to be looking at his maps, asking himself if all the engines suddenly stop and he has a fire, where is he going to land the plane in an emergency? It's no good him scrabbling around looking at the map when the plane's in flames. It's too late, you know. To maintain a business you have to be continually, almost daily, looking at the what ifs, how much can I lose and still maintain my obligations to creditors, what is my forward book, how secure is it, how can I cut my staff? If today I want to make a decision to cut my overheads and cut my costs, who are the first to go? Why will they go? How will I still do things? You have to be continually reviewing on an almost daily basis. I know, every day, my debtors, my creditors, my cash in the bank, my forward order book, my potential order book. I have eight different criteria and they get faxed to me wherever I am, every day. I go through myself the 'what if' scenario and try to encourage my management in the businesses to be doing it on a daily basis. I ring them up and test them, and say, what are you going to do if this doesn't happen next month – and I expect them to have a contingency plan. It's all about almost daily having contingency plans for the 'what if' factor.

And if it all goes wrong... deal with it. De Savary says:

The single most important thing that I discovered very early on is that when you know you've made a mistake, when you know it's going wrong, you put your hands up and admit it and at the same time try to make amends for it. Come up with a solution, come up with some way of compromising, do something to get out of the mistake. If you say that early on whoever you're dealing with on the other side, by and large, is understanding. What people are not understanding of is being misled, fooled, having the wool pulled over their eyes, having things concealed from them and later on, discovering that you could have told them this three months earlier, and if you'd done that maybe they could have solved the problem, maybe the problem wouldn't then be as bad.

I learnt very early on to put my hands up and say, 'We've made a mistake, we've got it wrong.' If you treat people with the respect they think they deserve, and probably do, they'll treat you that way. You could have made a mistake but have the courage and the energy to accept that if it does go wrong, you try as honourably as you can to rectify the situation, extricate yourself from the situation, and indeed, get up and have another go. Never feel defeated. Never give up.

10 THE LION'S DEN
Managing people

> There are two management styles that you can adopt for a person's weaknesses. You can either use it as a weapon against them or you can identify those weaknesses and support them and make the person a better individual… Never use a person's inadequacies as a weapon to improve their performance because you'll fail. You can't rule a company with fear.
>
> *Ron Dennis, head of McLaren International motor racing team.*

In 1991, the magazine *Management Week* carried a photograph of Ron Dennis on its cover with the question: 'Is Ron Dennis Britain's best manager?' McLaren is famous for its Formula One racing successes, but the bedrock of its business is management, and Ron Dennis – apart from being a brilliant technician – is a manager *par excellence.*

As he says himself, he could talk at length about the 'McLaren way', which permeates the pristine McLaren works at Woking, where visitors are invariably struck by the uncluttered, spotless, immaculate – it is tempting to say engineered – order of the place. Pass the seven gleaming F1 cars in the reception area and enter Dennis's office: there is not one single piece of paper to be seen except the one from which he is working. His impeccable appearance (razor cuffs, well-cut suit) reflect both his character and the ethic of the works, and it is a brief conversation with Dennis that fails to bring out both the engineer and the clarity of his thinking.

Not long before the Robert Half interview, the Chelsea chairman, Matthew Harding, had died in a helicopter crash. Dennis himself flies in helicopters frequently, and was asked, almost by way of introductory conversation, whether it had made him nervous of mechanical breakdown, which would lead a craft to plummet. Not at all, Dennis replied, firmly: it was clearly pilot error, since an engine failure would not have resulted in that sort of descent. His opinion was proved correct.

Focused, determined and disciplined are adjectives which attach to Dennis's management style; but with an organization of more than 700, the influence of the most charismatic, able boss needs corroboration and reinforcement from within the organization. How can this be done? In addressing that issue Dennis – in company with other subjects – returns to one key essential: however it is done, people have to constitute part of a team in which they can see their own contribution. There are subsidiary considerations: valuing staff, empowering them, creating 'micro-climates' if this means the individual is closer to the operation. Making it clear that they are relevant and valued is important and so is giving them a financial stake.

If de Savary is close to being a pure entrepreneur, Dennis, an engineer, is spoken of as an authority on pure management. It is a style, he says, which stemmed from Bruce McLaren, the McLaren founder. 'He was a very focused individual and in his time brought a sort of style, a determination, to achieving his own personal goals. I can't say that I necessarily inherited his style but the simple fact was he did leave some core values in the company. I supplemented those core values with my own style, which is a very focused style, and really built the company on changing values. As I matured as an individual and gained knowledge from a variety of sources, I was able to arrive at an ethos which saw everybody focused, very determined and disciplined. Inevitably, however, if you grow in size it becomes more and more difficult to maintain that and we've brought in different mechanisms to continually stimulate and motivate the work-force.'

Again, the answer lies in the team, Dennis says:

You shouldn't misunderstand the word. Of course, when we go to a Grand Prix there is a group of people and they're identified as the team, but they're very much the tip of the iceberg. One of the things you quickly learn if you're trying to run a successful Grand Prix organization is that there is always a gulf between the team – the people who go to the events – and the people who stay back. The Grand Prix organization is about 260 people, of which probably 50 of our own people go to each event.

Supplementing that are the spin-off companies where we've taken technologies that we've developed expertise in, formed those into separate business units, sometimes separate companies. So now we're around 700, growing at about 10 per cent a year, and every one of those 700 is part of the team.

The key is you've got to make everybody understand that they can contribute even if they're in a remote satellite company – contribute to the process of winning. Of course, winning's not just about winning Grands Prix. Winning is achieving every single goal that you set for the people to achieve. You could win as a person, you can win as an individual, you can win as a group, you can win as a company. Our objective is to be the best at everything, not just winning Grands Prix.

My style varies from company to company. I still have the luxury of going to Grands Prix, that's a relaxation for me, very much getting out of the office. It was also very much getting into a hands-on environment – be it that I never had a role. My role in the team doesn't exist – having said that, I'm very much immersed in strategy. I follow and tend to guide one of the cars at the Grands Prix, but very much in a 'papal' way. I don't actually physically engineer it but I obviously have quite a lot of experience, and therefore try to bring it to the process of winning.

It is a very constructive thing to stand up in front of the whole company and explain exactly what went on, and the pluses and the minuses and where we have to avoid making similar mistakes again. I accumulate, during the two weeks between the Grands Prix, various bits of information, and it also gives me an opportunity to communicate to the company as a whole. Sometimes it's good news, sometimes it's bad news, but I think it's better than a written memo or something on the notice board. If it's important enough it will be followed up with a more formal approach, but the starting point will always be looking into people's eyes and telling them exactly the way it is.

Dennis describes management as 'three-dimensional chess' which does not stop changing. McLaren, he says, tries different approaches:

When you get out into outposts of the company, the business culture's very different. We go through quite a complex and quite long process where each of the companies, and sometimes departments, are micro-climates – business micro-climates – where we're experimenting over a period of time, different ways to operate the company. The whole idea is to have a very defined plan for our new technology centre, which is a huge investment for us but will, I think, set new standards by which companies are run.

There are various styles and the easiest style is what I call domino management, where you look for a logical chain reaction and you use the structure of the company, especially if it's vertically integrated in the management layers, to communicate. The problem is that in some ways it's predictable, in other ways it doesn't create the stimulus that you can create if you move – not exactly against the structure that you've created, but by predicting a reaction, planning for the reaction and then instead of moving in a straight line, moving in a diagonal.

It isn't against the people who work for the company. People don't work for me, they work for the company, and I just happen to be the person that's managing the company at the moment. I think anybody who positions themselves as the beginning and the end of their organization is a pretty short-sighted individual. Apart from anything else, there comes a time when you're recruiting young people and you're approaching your mid, late fifties and they're asking themselves why they should put in 15, 20 years of their lives when this individual has not planned for the future.

I take very seriously trying to convey to everybody that I'm not it, I'm just it at the moment. The whole process of management is about responsibility, accountability, all the way to the top. I have things that I am accountable [for]. I'm accountable to my conscience. I'm accountable to my co-shareholder, which is an easy ride because we're a successful business, which is by far what I prefer – so if anyone's going to applaud the results of my efforts it's as a businessman, not as a sportsman.

The virtue of the team is a belief that emerges again and again. Greg Dyke went to Harvard – but most of what he knows about management, he says, was learned in one concentrated period, when he was putting together the *Six O'Clock Show* for London Weekend. And if not a team, then a variation on it – as Dyke found when working 'on instinct' at TV-am. Bringing together a rag-bag of egos, it was a task, he says, to try to instil a sense of 'family' when there can be such an atmosphere of competition. 'If you can create them as a family, it will work,' he says.

To Jack Rowell – Rowell the great coach, as well as Rowell the businessman – life's a team, and the technique for success is to inspire, to train, then to hand over the reins. His philosophy once was to be 'pushy and hard', but later he became convinced that what he calls 'head room' is vital. Once out on a field, a team has to be its own manager:

> There is no bigger demand for a self-managed team than a rugby team. They've got to play on their own. Soccer managers are shouting instructions all the time, but there are so many problems for rugby players to solve on the hoof that we want them to have empowerment to solve the problems. That's one of the key success factors. We ask men to differentiate near to the edge, and that they are confident in their own business. We played one team when I was in Bath in the final, and Bath won when they shouldn't have done. Afterwards they said to me, 'We've just been talking to the opposition and asked why they lost and they said they'd have to go and ask the coach.' I said, 'Can you imagine asking a Bath player that?' They'd take offence, and that's as it should be. It's the same in business – you want empowered individuals, which means you do not just say 'You're empowered', but give them head room, back up with proper training and skills, and build the team out of self-relying individuals.

Competition, Rowell says, is essential – 'Human nature says that if you become successful you might sit on your laurels. What you want is competition for places, as well as getting people queuing up, ready to take over.'

Then there are egos, which can militate against working for the team. They also have to be managed:

> It's not all about high-powered individuals, although you do need them. It's about team work, and to me the best team wins. What you're looking for is a blend of skills, a blend of personalities who get on with each other. That's quite often hard – particularly in sports teams, when the egos are so high, and they've got to be to put up with the pressure they're under. They're bound to forget the self-sacrifice that good team work demands. That's a big factor, and the big players flaunt it. [Putting together a good team] is blending, getting people to understand the give and take, accepting as a player that it's not all about high-power delivery. It certainly needs some team work and a system of play.

As a boss (and/or a coach), Rowell says, it is an enormous mistake to try to make your team dependent on you. The parallels between sport and commerce are legitimate:

On a rugby field, certain people go on 90 minutes, and they can deal with anything the opposition throws at them, or the conditions or the crowds or whatever. On the hoof, they can cope rather than being coach-dependent. They need to be as self-reliant as is possible, and the confidence that gives them. Where you've got a team more self-reliant than the opposition that is a winning edge in itself and a good driving force, because the players get a lot out of that. After games they analyse on their own what went right, what went wrong, what we need to look at. Before the game I keep out of the dressing room for half an hour so they feel in it together and stand against the rest of the world. And [so that they] feel relaxed. So they're tactically good but very strong-minded too.

Individuals cannot be managed in the same way:

Some people need pushing, some need pulling, some need a touch on the withers. What it isn't, for sure, is a pep talk before the game. Although that is a powerful weapon, that would be a veneer really. If your business were a shambles you'd need the leader, the coach, the manager, the chief executive, whatever. The more the team comes together, the more I think you want to really withdraw because teams, if they feel that they're doing it themselves, are more committed and will achieve more. So – control where it's a shambles, but the opposite when it isn't, so they feel very positive that they own the strategy.

Ron Dennis has stressed the importance of 'micro-climates' in keeping any venture on a scale which individuals can identify with. Prue Leith concurs wholly with this. After she had sold her business (to a French company) she watched its new owners put in more centralized systems and – almost simultaneously – their profits fall:

I believe the answer is to keep subdividing into small profit centres and not to try to centralize anything. When I originally sold the business I thought that as it was to a French company I could go on doing what I'd always done. I was a bit naïve. They wanted to expand right over England and were using us as their spearhead, and they thought they had better centralize everything and put a lot of control in – marketing department, sales department, big glossy brochures. Not to mince words, we were a very profitable company when they bought us; they paid a lot of money for us and within a year we were not a profitable company and it looked as if they had wasted the money.

When big companies take over small companies they should be concerned to keep the value. Not all our managers stayed. We had the usual problem. They still enjoy what they are doing but because of their entrepreneurial bent, they can't stand the dead weight of bureaucracy and upward requests and downward approval and committees and meetings – so they just leave. They think, 'This is boring, it's not fun' – so they leave. And then – guess what? – the clients leave, the profits leave, everything leaves.

Once the team is in place, the next issue is how to motivate its members. Peter de Savary, whose personality comes into the room before him, tries to almost infect his staff with a sense of the excitement that he feels about his projects. Less enigmatically, he makes it very clear that he values their contribution:

I try to instil in all those I work with – and without them I wouldn't be doing anything – a sense of adventure and a sense of pioneering and above all, a sense of pride. The most exciting news I've had all week is that, as I was arriving in the car, I got a call on the wretched beastly mobile phone (which I think should probably be banned), telling me that our young chef at Skibo Castle in Scotland has just won the award as young chef of the year, which is a great honour in the very northern Highlands. Within a few minutes I got a second call that said we had also won the chef of the year award. The excitement that we have those two awards is not for the club and the business and for me, but for those two young people up there in the Highlands. What a great achievement. How proud they must feel and proud we must all feel. And I told my secretary immediately, send a fax to all 517 members of the Carnegie Club, right now, giving them the good news. It's that sort of attitude that makes us all enjoy it.

The ability to enthuse can be worked at. It can also be reinforced with physical devices (money being one of them, although not necessarily the most important). Reward is implicit in people management. Sir Terence Conran says financial reward can be deferred as long as enthusiasm is engendered: 'You've got to be a very good team-builder and enthuser, because you have to have around you people probably who are not going to be paid very much, but must believe in you and your ideas and believe that they will eventually get good rewards.'

Chris Wright, discussing changing the culture at Queens Park Rangers, echoes that commitment has to come from the top:

> If the chairman doesn't care, why should the receptionist care? You have to instil that we will do well, care that we will be successful on the pitch, care that we win, because winning is very important, and you have to send that message out very loud and very clear. I hope that I made a fairly immediate impact, that that was an important thing to do right from the start.

Prue Leith says managers must also remember how hard it can be at the bottom:

> I'm very sympathetic to young people coming into the business. I think we forget what agony it is on the first day, because you're so tired and so tense. It's a very scary thing. I try very hard to make sure that our people are looked after. I reckon that if you make the first three days enjoyable in any job, there is a good chance you will keep those people. They always say in aeroplanes that the first two minutes are critical – I reckon the first three days in any job are critical.

Just before David Lloyd sold out to Whitbread, he was managing 18 centres and 40,000 staff. One of his techniques was in making shares in the business available to the staff. Another was to give each centre control over its own affairs:

> The clubs are autonomous – they run them. Every manager does his own budget, sets it, head office sets membership fees and we have a central purchasing unit where we set the prices of buying and selling. His bonus at the end of the year is on three things: operating line, member-

ship line, but most importantly, customer care line. If he doesn't make his percentage on the list rated by the mystery shopper [anonymous visitors who marked the club against a set of criteria] he gets nothing.

Lloyd also motivated his staff by giving them openings to move up, especially tennis pros moving into management. 'I encourage the pros who are a little younger to look at management. They know their members better than anybody, and that's important, because the manager has to be out there meeting the customers. They're bright people and they need a career that goes on past 45.'

As Prue Leith says, people also have to feel trusted as well as relevant and valued:

> The essentially important thing about business is trust, not just that the window cleaner is going to clean the windows, or that the Dover sole isn't lemon sole, but trust of employees to do their work. We all trust our PAs, so why don't we trust our managers? The most important thing is to hire the right people in the first place and then to give them trust, not just this great 'empowerment' jargon stuff. There is a lot of talk about accountability, responsibility, empowerment – to a lot of people it looks like an excuse for catching you out, and probably 'de-layering' you... I'm all for counting in and counting out and proper stock control, but to assume everybody is going to be a crook and putting in so much control, not only do you waste administrative money, but you demotivate the person.

Which takes us to the rocky road of recruitment. What do you look for? Leith is sure of one potential employee a boss should certainly avoid: someone whom they dislike on sight. When it comes to relying on gut instinct, the subjects agree that this is one field where it should not be ignored.

Leith says: 'I have been saying for years that I think nobody should ever hire anybody they don't want to have lunch with. Why spend eight hours of your life with people you don't like? I don't mean you should hire clones – we all like people who are very different from ourselves – but don't hire people you don't like, and don't hire people you don't think you're going to trust.' Sir Terence Conran puts it slightly differently, but has exactly the same view. His first criterion in recruiting is to ask whether he simply likes the person.

David Lloyd describes himself as 'probably the worst interviewer of all time'. If he does not like the individual in front of him, he knows he will not be able to work with them. 'I sit down and ask one question and I either like the guy or don't like the guy. That's it, really, because at the end of the day if I don't like him there's no point, and if he doesn't like me, there's no point either. I ask what's your name, anything, just to look him in the face. I don't go into detail. I just like to see if I like the chap or not.'

This vital question over, the next big consideration is how much that person is empathetic with the organization. Lloyd says:

> Once we get beyond the first question, I'm looking for someone who's really going to have pride in the company, willing to make decisions and make mistakes and come back again, but to try 100 per cent. There is no short-cut to trying. The same thing applies in tennis. The game has changed and the McEnroes of this world – and he's the greatest player I have seen – are rare. Agassi is another exception, but I don't think there are many 'racquet talent' people making it to number one. It's the Lendls, the Chrises (Evert) and the guys who are putting in the hours on the court. Nothing gets in the way, they are totally dedicated, nothing upsets them from this task. I think it's the same in business. You really do need this blinkered vision and hard work and dedication, and heart.
>
> I'm not saying the financial manager has to learn where the foul sewer is, but you've got to be part of the team, get to know the managers, find out how the business ticks from the manager level. I'm looking at all the people that can actually do a bit of everything. The whole concept of the company is that we can all mix in and do each other's jobs. [When I was looking for a financial manager] I was not looking for somebody who sat in his office and dictated orders all the way down the line; he actually had to do something hands-on in the company.

Prue Leith once ruled out a potential managing director on the strength of what he ordered for lunch. Seated in her Michelin-starred restaurant, he waved away the menu and ordered a steak:

> I thought, 'You can leave now,' and I was right, because he was absolutely impossible. He would have had no idea that he had written himself out of the job in the first place because he thought the most important thing was his background in accounts and the fantastic profits he had made for somebody else, and how he had turned the company round. But if you don't like what you're selling... to be in the food

business, you have to be greedy! If you ever applied for a job in any form with us you would probably be asked by any of our managers where you liked to eat. You wouldn't want an Avon lady not to wear make-up, would you, or not to care about bath salts?

Anita Roddick demands more than an interest in cosmetics when The Body Shop recruits its franchisees:

People know before they come into The Body Shop what it stands for, that there's another agenda there other than the trading agenda. That is that we are a campaigning company and a consciousness-raising company. Everybody sees we have a mission statement, which is very radical. We have two-way assessments where the juniors in a department would actually interview the people who have been recruited, so it's not just peers. We don't do anything psychological. One thing I do use, especially with franchisees, is a particular questionnaire, with questions such as, 'What are you most proud of?' and 'Who are your heroes in history?' We ask them two questions which are really quite important: 'What car do you have, and what car would you like to have?' If it jumps from a clapped out VW Golf to a Maserati, we are going to have real problems with them. They come for an interview, sit down with juniors as well as their own peer group and think, 'God, I'm being asked questions by the tea lady!'

Barry Hearn relies on his instinct to such an extent that he has been agent for some sportsmen for years without a contract existing. Hearn managed Steve Davis for 20 years while Jimmy White left and came back. Hearn says his management style, and the way he takes on sportsmen, had to change as the politics and finances of televised sport altered, but it was not always possible to effect the change:

When we were in the snooker early on we were pals, we were making bundles of money, the world was our oyster. There wasn't competition out on the playing surface so we were winning everything and everybody got complacent, me included. I saw the writing on the wall but it was impossible to change certain of my players' attitudes. They thought they were invincible. They thought they were always going to earn three, four or five hundred thousand pounds a year. Unfortunately new kids come in the gate and they can't beat them. When a youngster comes into a playing field with no worries, just wants to play, wants to win, these are dangerous bastards. They've got nothing else on their minds. What happened was that they [established players] eventually started getting beaten.

Managing top sports personalities can have its own demands, beyond the usual call of duty of any manager. Hearn's brief was so wide that it was, he says, more akin to baby-sitting (Chris Wright had a similar experience with his bands). Rick Parry's task in gaining consensus from 20 football club chairmen required skills he was not even sure he had, believing, in the beginning, that every day could be his last.

But while much of management can be broken down into key principles, there will always be room for the unorthodox and unconventional approach. Sometimes, the business itself requires a mix of thick skin and genius, or sensitivity and hunches... as Chris Wright says, management in football and in music can be a matter of betting on an unknown quantity. There is the textbook way to carry out a transaction, and then there is the only way possible in the circumstances at that moment – and there can be two very different outcomes:

> Of the 92 clubs in the Premier League and the Football League, there are probably about six trading as they should be from a proper traditional corporate standpoint. The rest of them are trying to get to the point that they can do that, and I think it's very difficult. You are making decisions all the time which, in a proper financially controlled environment you would probably not be making. It's very very difficult. You have to somehow try to marry the two, and in a way it's similar to the record business. Within Chrysalis we have a variety of different businesses. Some can budget very effectively and some can't, because when you sign a group to a record deal or a publishing deal, you're paying four guys or girls who have never made a record – sometimes never appeared on stage – and you pay them a lot of money in the expectation they may be successful. You can't budget for success, but you have to say, right, we'll do it.

Compared with managing rock bands, however, Wright has found football painless. He gave up being a manager because whatever happened, it was always the manager's fault. There is not one single commercial principle of any use when a prima donna (of either sex) is throwing either a tantrum or large pieces of furniture around a hotel suite. There are some jobs too hot to handle:

> The manager's job is very much to baby-sit. If you're the record company, they might complain and whinge, but basically they get a cheque from you every six months. If you're the music publisher they get a cheque from you every six months, but if you are the manager, whoever the cheque goes to, they're paying you. They pay you whatever it is – 10 per cent, 15 per cent, 20 per cent of whatever it is they earn. Basically, the manager is obviously worth what he's making, because he's generally making that income for them, but they're still paying the manager, so they expect the manager to be available to do whatever. Baby-sitting is part of it, and it doesn't make any difference, it's a 24-hour-a-day, seven-days-a-week role. If the drummer's wife doesn't get a seat next to him on the aeroplane that's your fault, it doesn't matter where you are in the world, you get on the phone and complain.
>
> In the case of Ten Years After, I think I had to keep a group together there who would have broken up after day one if hadn't been for me. They were always fighting, and actually fist fighting on stage some of the time. There was one bit with Ten Years After where they did a number called 'Good Morning Little School Girl' and it was one of the highlights of the set, where the keyboard player and the drummer basically stopped and the guitarist and the bass player riffed next to each other. There were several nights where they were standing face to face, I can't repeat what they were saying, and the guitars were swinging, their heads were ducking. To get them to go on stage when they've had a row and you have 20,000 people out there and someone is saying 'I'm never working with him again'... it can be quite strenuous.

Peter de Savary's management style is not taken from any rule book:

> Part of the attraction for me of being an entrepreneur is that it's a very emotional thing. There's a lot of you, a lot of your energy, a lot of your personality and a great deal of your emotion in it. And you have to transmit that to your colleagues, to your partners, to your staff, to your bankers, to your advisers. And you have to bring them into that emotion and get them also, to some degree, to have a soul. And if you can do that there's a better chance of success. It's a lot more fun. It's a lot more enjoyable. Perhaps sometimes the financial gain isn't as great but the overall satisfaction is much better.

Anita Roddick has the same view. The Body Shop, a liberal, informal, first-name-terms institution, has been described as very un-British. Roddick herself calls it 'a benign dictatorship':

> It is important because when you have – as in America – 33 competitors, they see something and they plagiarize it as best they can as there is no way you can start watering down the corporate image or the logo. There are many areas that are sacrosanct – the colour green and the typeface. All that control is on every level of production development. That's not to say that wonderful ideas don't come in from the franchisees. We have extraordinarily benevolent meetings about their ideas and what they want. Autonomy comes in how they manage their sense of real connection with the staff, how they do their public relations.

More fundamentally, it is a personal reflection of Anita and Gordon Roddick, for whom the personal and professional blend into one:

> About four years ago we thought we had to have someone in the house to help. My mum was doing the washing. I said OK, let's get a couple in just to clear up – and they fired us! They fired us because I didn't wear a hat when I got the OBE and she was so devastated, this woman. We have people to help us in our house who are like New Zealand travellers. We're informal because it's the family, but it's too big for a family, so it's a bit like a community. And there are babies: we had the child development centre attached to the work-place. You have babies there and they go through the company handing out their little organic apples to you. How can you be formal? I don't know how to be different.

Not only would she fail to be any different, Roddick says, she believes that the personal nature of The Body Shop has helped in its success:

> The strategy I have is to keep that entrepreneurial thinking, in protecting it like a lion would protect its cubs. Because I'm a bit more high profile and on television, or whatever, there's a sort of guardedness that can creep in. You've got to break that down, so at every level I'm in with the staff. I stay in their homes when I travel. I'm doing things with them so that I can challenge their notion of what business should be about. It's all about embracing and praising and having this convivial sense of touching, knowing your stuff. It really does work.

The approach militates against that time-honoured time-waster: the meeting. Roddick says:

> Meetings are turgid. Meetings are an excuse to do nothing: the same people say the same old thing. So I usually scupper the meetings; I scuppered one yesterday. The big guns came – there is still a lot of testosterone in our company – and wanted to talk, and they hadn't got a clue what they were talking about – brand instead of range. So I bring in a product development team and we throw in all the new logos and all the new branding that is bigger and they suddenly realize – you know, through a bit of theatre and getting out of their bloody rooms, which they never do – that they have to have more respect for the people that are looking after the company.

One potential drawback of this management style, however, is that it can lead to a volatile work-place. The Body Shop staff work off their frustrations in the cloakrooms and vent their anger with the aid of red envelopes, as Roddick explains:

> There are two areas of real empowerment: the lavatory is one. Loos are great ways of giving information, whether you put things on the wall or ask for comments. You write things on the wall anonymously.
>
> The other thing we have is a red envelope which comes with the employment manual, which is wonderful. Each person is given loads of envelopes and any time they are bugged with anything we do they write directly to the board, or member of the board, and the board has to answer within 24 hours. This is brilliant for defusing problems and keeps the board in touch with the real thinking of the real people who do the real work in the company. And we send our staff off. We give them sabbaticals and they go to places like Romania and Albania and Russia, working in orphanages and working in mental institutions, so their measurement is not just productivity like a TQM measurement, but the productivity of the human spirit. It is measured by how they treat the weak and the frail, and they come back as enhanced, challenging human beings.

Despite arriving in general consciousness as 'the caring Nineties', the culture at work has not followed this trend. Is this a positive thing? Lord Sheppard oversaw thousands of redundancies in his efforts to streamline the organizations he was managing – we shall look at this later – and gained a reputation as formidable boss who believed in management through a 'loose grip on the throat'. Prue Leith rages against the machismo culture of long hours, which she says are destructive, dishonest and unnecessary. Jack Rowell and Ron Dennis talk of the weakness of fear as a management tool.

Yet none of these people is known as a pussy cat, any more than Anita Roddick is regarded as a green softie. On the contrary. Effective managers do not rule through fear. But they recognize that there have to be benchmarks of failure present in any organization. They also believe that relationships should be simple and direct, which may be perceived as alarming.

Leith's organization adopted the motto 'Simply Better' to reflect the straightforwardness of its approach. Ron Dennis's organization is based on precision. Human error always emerges, but Dennis says that how it is dealt with is what determines whether the experience is instructive or destructive:

> There are two management styles that you can adopt for a person's weaknesses. You can either use it as a weapon against them or you can identify those weaknesses and support them and make the person a better individual. When people make mistakes you've always got to make that judgement. I never judge and I never use a person's inadequacies as a weapon to improve their performance – it will fail. You cannot rule a company with fear. Although you see it all the time, you will not find it in our company anywhere. If an individual makes a mistake, the environment that we've created is one where the pain he feels, just by making a mistake, is far greater than anything I can exert on him. You don't stand him up in front of the company and say 'This guy made a mistake'. Everybody knows. What we do is analyse right down – and we have tremendous systems. If any component fails on our racing car anywhere in the world we can tell you from what drawing it was made, from what material it was made, what date it was made, how many miles it's done, how many hours it's done. We can give you – and there's about 3,000-odd components on a racing car – what batch it was made from etc, and then the processes.
>
> Whenever there is a failure or mistake, we can trace it right back to source very, very accurately, and that individual knows and then he's got to learn from it. It's really like the sum of the total or the weakest link; the role of management is always to try to identify the weakest links and support them and strengthen them. Mistakes are part of management, are part of any company and you've got to take a mistake and turn it into a positive. It's very easy, in our environment, to accept mis-

takes because everybody makes them, including myself. You just expose them for what they are – mistakes, and you try to make sure they don't happen again by introducing systems. It's rarely the company or the systems or the procedures that are at fault when we make mistakes. It's because an individual's dropped off. We have covering situations too so it doesn't happen often.

Jack Rowell was long associated with using a fear factor. So it comes as a surprise that he won't hear of it. 'You don't want to lose your job, do you? And that's a fear factor. People don't want to be left out of teams. You don't threaten them or anything like that. What most people want is to succeed, and that is a main driving force whether we like it or not.'

Rowell does, however, believe in peer pressure to motivate a good side and they must recognize that their ego comes second to the team. And peer approval, Rowell says, is as powerful as peer pressure:

Players are very professional; they set standards and they will have a go at people who don't get there. They'll turn on the manager if they need to, as well. If he's up to it they'll say, 'These are our standards, toe the line and get up there or you're not one of us.'

Rowell told the *Sunday Telegraph* in 1995: 'I recruit self-driven and competitive people, then I can challenge an individual. After that it becomes a mutual challenge between him and me. People who aren't driven find that uncomfortable. They become marginalized very quickly.'

Rowell's management technique has never been called soft, but it does not lack subtlety. Adapting to the very different individuals requires skill but principally, it requires persuading them to 'share a vision': 'When we got to Scotland the theme was to show the video of people doing famous things in the England team while the music "Search for the hero inside yourself" played. Beyond that, you know, you need to be personal. We had bad times as well as good ones and we needed to stick behind them, which we did.'

Rowell's mantra is 'preparation, organization, communication' – they, he says, are the tools through which players can be motivated to pursue high standards, not just for the one-off international but, as in the case of Bath, week after week:

If you say to Bath you ought to be the best in the country and it's rational, people will believe it. That's a great motivational thing. Preparation, organization, communication... very importantly, the players themselves do most of the talking. It is personal words, players knowing where they stand and what they need to do to get better. And to value them.

Prue Leith's belief in directness has been known to come unstuck – notably when she rehearsed a tactful speech of dismissal then blurted out 'You're fired!' as her disastrous employee clomped up the stairs to her office – but on the whole, she hates false illusions. Working long hours, she maintains, is one of the worst:

I think it is nonsense, the hours we work – you work, I don't work. It's a conspiracy to prevent women getting to the top. I was at a plc [company] board meeting a little while ago because I was leading the initiative Opportunity 2000 to get women into management. We started discussing hours of work and I said it would be a very good idea if the board went home at 5.30 because until the board goes home at 5.30, nobody else is going to do it. It would stop chaps leaving their jackets on the back of the chair so they could pretend they hadn't gone home. It would stop young men in particular getting into work before the boss so they could get Brownie points. It would stop women feeling guilty because they had to go home to the children. Everyone should do a decent day's work but not more. And we all know that people don't work that well after more than about eight or nine hours work, which is unfair to women as they are thought of as not committed.

I have some good evidence of this from a survey. We had asked all the senior managers in a particular company to evaluate their middle management, which was about 50 per cent women and 50 per cent men, on all the usual performance indicators, leadership, results, confrontation skills, and the women middle management had scored slightly better than the men, about 4 per cent better. About five weeks later we went back to them and asked them to look at the same people and recommend them for recruitment. The women did 15 per cent worse than the men in spite of performing better. When questioned further the senior managers – all men – said: 'We couldn't promote her; she's not committed. She goes home.' I was then talking to a woman senior executive about this. She said: 'It's absolutely par for the course. The fact is that men get promoted for taking 11 hours a day to do something that we do better in eight.'

Leith suggested to the board that it would be better if the men could have a more normal life – they thought she didn't understand the way of business. None of the men with children would speak out for fear of being thought a wimp, although a couple told her she was right in the corridor afterwards, and said the reason they didn't go home was that they were exhausted from early mornings:

> One of them said: 'What really winds me up is when I get into my car at 6.30 in the morning and there's a message on the car phone answerthing from my boss and it says, 'Hi, John. It's 6.15 (am). Just thought I might catch you, but give me a ring when you get in.' We all know what that means – 'I was in my car before you were in your car.' I don't believe that women go in for such stressful power games, they must think it's garbage. I'm not saying for a second that there aren't times in a company's life when you have to work all the hours that God sends. But I don't believe there's a man in this room who can put his hand on his heart and say that every hour he stays in the office is necessary.

Long hours? It must be time to bring in Lord Sheppard – not only a self-confessed workaholic but voted, in a *Sunday Times* poll in 1993, Britain's toughest boss. Is he so fearsome? He has a passion for helping people to help themselves. This led him to initiate the GrandMet Trust, which has trained over 300,000 people since 1982, previously unemployed, for jobs. It also led to him being chairman of Business in the Community and of the Prince's Trust, both deeply involved in helping young people in need. Sheppard himself says it is understandable that he was thus labelled, considering the dramatic changes he and his board colleagues instituted at GrandMet:

> GrandMet has very much got a challenge culture, for all types of reasons, and once you start getting that you obviously attract like people. It began, I guess, with Maxwell Joseph, the founder chairman, who had a very low boredom threshold and wasn't remotely interested in anything managerial. So if you spoke to him for about a minute on a management subject you could see him switch off completely. As a result the whole of Grand Met had a very low boredom threshold. We didn't spend a lot of time writing to each other but talked through issues. It is a genuine challenge culture that we had, which is linked in with that kind of style, whereby

people were expected – at every level – to be challenged and to challenge. All our management training programmes involved a proposal to the board of what the board had done wrong in the previous 12 months, and it was circulated to the whole board. And we actually gave them an answer to their questions and met them face to face six months later.

GrandMet meetings were called 'rowdy'.

We genuinely did make decisions at board meetings. As we know, a lot of boards actually use them to rubber stamp. As chief executive I would go into a meeting with quite a clear view but not necessarily expecting to come out of the debate with this unchanged. The guy running food may express a strong anti view or positive view on something to do with drinks. In this way he'd be there in the same way as a non-exec. So we had a real debate and there wouldn't be a situation where the executive committee had a view and then sold it to the non-execs.

But rather than a 'loose grip' close to the jugular, he prefers the expression 'orchestrated anarchy' for his preferred style:

Management has got to work in the Nineties by having really top quality people – better than yourself, preferably. To give them absolute authority to do what they consider correct, working within an ethical frame and a strategic frame. Therefore it's up to the management – this is true of whatever levels there are, and there shouldn't be many levels! – to orchestrate that flair and drive to get the maximum product out of it. That's what management's about, orchestrating that drive from the people who really know, the people on the factory floor and those who know the customer.

Over a decade in industry, Sheppard was also at the helm when thousands of redundancies were made. Did he think 'downsizing' had become an epidemic? On the contrary:

If there is a criticism to be made, it is that it was carried out too slowly. In the early Eighties, when there was a huge round of reductions, we'd all become, without realizing it, heavily institutionalized. This included governments of all types and colours as well as businesses. Suddenly the UK realized that we'd been chronically overmanned. We were looking at 5 per cent improvements and we needed to be looking at 50 per cent improvements. That was one rude awakening and I think by and large what was done there was correct.

In the early Nineties, the issues at GrandMet were different. We'd done all the 'easy' things, we'd cut the head count by a massive amount. You had to really start all over again from a blank sheet to achieve greater efficiency. If you take Burger King, just for an example. The day we arrived, there were 13 levels of management between the president and the guy actually serving the burgers. Within three months we made that seven levels of management, which was quite a lot of reorganization. The industry thought we'd gone mad and had got it wrong and – in fact – they were right. We hadn't cut it enough. We'd cut the levels more two years later. That was 1988–9 but in 1993–4, the Burger King people themselves started, as with all of our businesses, to re-engineer. What they did was to start considering what businesses we were really in. These were selling franchises and selling burgers, Coca-Cola and fries and all the other sophistications are irrelevant really. That led them to go right the way through and restructure the whole of the business from the top and take out yet another third of the people whilst putting more into the front line to improve service. Certainly, in the case of GrandMet, if I had any criticism – and it's easy to have hindsight – we were too slow. Media comment was 'Why are they taking out people they've only just put in?' But some people had been there for a hundred years – I'm exaggerating – it should always be, not how you do it 10 per cent better, but how do you do it entirely differently. That's what we did with every one of our businesses.

Take a different example to that on, say, factories: the whole examination of 'do we actually need supervision' took out rafts of supervisory staff. And 'do you actually need management of plants'. We actually got to the stage of running several of our seasonal plants without a permanent management while they worked intensively for four months. You could do it by shifting people from a kind of mother-house out to the satellites for just that part of the year. Meanwhile, you just wanted a middle management just to make certain somebody wasn't stealing the whole of the factory or something like that. So it's really fundamental thinking of doing things entirely differently.

Sheppard was a bold manager, becoming known for his 'magic numbers' – goals which could not be achieved by any logic or even any means, other than by guts and belief. If these aims could not be achieved, they inculcated a culture of high aims:

Magic numbers is really part of not accepting the impossible is impossible. It means numbers which in logic you cannot add up, you know you cannot get the answer you want. Therefore it's really to do with thinking the impossible and saying how you're going to succeed – how are you going to run a business not with 10 per cent less head count but with 60 per cent less head count. Or how you're going to double your market share rather than put it up by 1 per cent. There is no logic behind this other than guts and quality of people. In the end, the expression worked into the GrandMet system – it wasn't just me, but other people picking up the same concept.

Ambitious plans involving a significant contribution from staff, however, demand that something be given by the company as well. Sheppard and David Lloyd say that no organization reliant on its people should expect them to perform without training.

A failure to realize this in the beginning was one of Lloyd's biggest mistakes, which he corrected. 'The clubs were all rated by the mystery shoppers and by questionnaires from the members and were awarded points. They have a league table and I had some very competitive managers. They were on the phone saying to each other, "How come you got 10 for catering?" It was terrific, built up by team spirit amongst their own unit. They got awards, trips and financial gain by doing it.'

Sheppard says a failure to train is a short-cut to total failure and that it should be 'absolutely mainstream' – not an afterthought:

Management should realize that unless they're going to make the best use of skills and work on improving the skills – through concepts such as learning for life – of everybody in their organization, then they're on a pretty short time fuse. Unless you actually get that philosophy into the company at every level – not just the HR function but everywhere – then it doesn't work. It can't be an add-on, it's got to be part of the mainstream thinking of the company. The other thing you've got to do, as part of that training, is to have a system of proper management development which clearly identifies people's skills and needs and shifts people around who want to be shifted around.

11 ALL CHANGE
Coping with change

I think that the consumer, especially the modern consumer, does not want a brand thrust in their face. It's a more subtle sell now... I'm either awfully right or awfully wrong

Ron Dennis, managing director of TAG McLaren,
most successful racing team of all time.

Change is part of any career, whether it be cultural, commercial, strategic or the career itself. It may be the change involved when an idiosyncratic, private company decides to go to the Stock Exchange. It may be when an individual senses that social change will affect the way he or she operates. It often involves other people (which is where the equation gets particularly complex).

All our subjects have experienced change. The nature of their experiences is very different, but one common factor emerges: change can be painful, stressful and expensive and it often has casualties. It can mean losing in the short term to gain in the longer term and, sometimes, it takes on a nature of its own which may not be a welcome alteration. Occasionally, when the plunge has been taken and the water found too inhospitable, it has been necessary to walk away.

Jack Rowell found himself in the centre of the radical culture change in rugby: from amateurism to professionalism. It was a change, he says, which he regrets but saw as inevitable:

I think that's where rugby's got to, I would say regretfully. Rugby's hard, and hence I think its ongoing ethos and popularity is that it was a man's game and a wonderful game from my point. I'm in it because I enjoy the people as well as the player managing – it's instant society.

But increasingly, I think what has driven rugby union to professionalism is the fact that you've got to train five days a week, perhaps more, perhaps a little less, but something like that, and it is a huge time commitment. What people were doing was working during the day and doing that training in addition. The southern hemisphere has seen this before the northern hemisphere and said the game's got to go professional. They took the initiative, which everyone else had to follow. So we're now in that, but before that there was nothing wrong with the way it was run. We now have to find the money. We're searching for the next professional game at the top level, but still a game for everyone to participate in at their own particular level and enjoy.

Rowell expects rugby to come out the other side with some bad decisions having been made at speed, but for the game to survive with its parts intact. There are, he maintains, parallels between the best practice in a sporting scenario and a business situation. It is crucial to communicate with everyone involved and explain the case for change:

> Communication is a critical issue for one thing. I've been in other businesses and companies with the biggest turnaround, a vast change. To change the culture takes a while and that is critical, but people need to understand the need.
>
> What I did find in businesses was that one may have some doubt about the need for a change management programme and you need to think that through. Segregating the areas of change, selling it, involving people. People don't like change, everyone is conservative and the chief executive or the rugby coach have really got to sit down and work through the whys and wherefores. When I got involved with England to start with I said I feel we needed change for these reasons. We had a couple of games a year the previous autumn, one against Canada and before that against Romania, and we scored over 50 points in each. The message that needed selling was that we needed flexibility. We'd been on a tour to South Africa earlier in that summer and they saw then that the way England played traditionally wouldn't work in the southern hemisphere. So they saw the reasons, they got involved and implemented it on the field. That's my best example. It is identifying where you want to be, each individual change involved, getting the people to want the change, and being involved with it. Communication is paramount. One cannot over-communicate.

Chris Wright, who established Loftus Road plc to buy Queens Park Rangers and set about changing it from a family-owned organization to a commercial business, says commitment to change has to come from the top, and everyone involved has to see that senior management is involved heart and soul.

> Changing for long-term advantage is peppered with set-backs. There is often a resistance to appearing to want to mend what is not broken, thus ensuring that broken it surely will be.

The share price of GrandMet sank, and stayed depressed for a long time, when chief executive Lord Sheppard and his colleagues on the board decided that they had to change it from a rag-bag of businesses with no common ground to a focused group in a chosen commodity. GrandMet had started in hotels but grew into a broadly based conglomerate. When it decided to divest itself of unrelated businesses and to focus on international food and drinks brands, commentators thought the board had taken leave of their senses. The board saw it rather as major strategic action on a business that was in a state of confusion and needed to focus on its core skills. Sheppard says:

> I'd been there 11 years when I became group chief executive. GrandMet was a very successful company. It had been set up in 1962 and it had grown massively. The policy that the founder chairman, Maxwell Joseph, and his lieutenants had followed was to have no policy other than success. It was very much a conglomerate and it ended up in about 28 different businesses. So we weren't turning round the business but ensuring it had a future. It also lacked a common culture. We had to think through what we really were.
>
> There were probably about a dozen of us who were involved in the process to try to understand what each of us thought GrandMet was. We were trying to understand what the core skills of GrandMet were. Were we just lucky? How did GrandMet add value, did we add value? We used two consultants, not to tell us what to do but to talk to. Obviously, we had to continue to work with each other so they then fed

us back a kind of stripped-down version of what we'd all said about each other. The fact of it was that at that time, we didn't have much idea of how we added value.

Before I became chief executive we'd had a study done on the future of the hotel business. We owned Intercontinental with about 100 hotels worldwide, and had reached the conclusion that it was quite difficult at that stage, as we could see it, for a publicly quoted company to get the earnings gross that were necessary to stay alive in the hotel business. At that stage property was going straight through the roof – this was the late Eighties – and we were fearful that there would be a property downswing which would obviously have taken hotels right down with it. So we reached the conclusion, as a board, that we should exit hotels – which was quite difficult because it was where we'd begun.

The board concluded that GrandMet's strengths were international marketing skills, and pure operational skills. It also had good financial disciplines. Sheppard was accused of being on some form of ego trip, but communicating was difficult. As Sheppard says, 'You can't stand up publicly and say "we're going to try and double the profits of this business and then flog it" – the hotel business is people driven and we needed to keep up motivation.'

GrandMet decided to build on its wine and spirits, international and heavily branded, and also to bank on the food industry going the same way over the coming decades:

We had to start building up our food business. We had two initial targets, Rowntree in the UK and Pillsbury in the States. Rowntree would have been easier because we could have used paper whereas we had to do it all with debt in the States, but while we were pondering Rowntree was taken over. So we were left with Pillsbury, which turned out to be the right decision for us.

Having taken the plunge, GrandMet then faced the task of changing the culture of Pillsbury, a relatively conservative organization. GrandMet had limited knowledge on food (it owned Express Dairies and a US dog food business). 'The real test was whether we could instil into Burger King, and into Pillsbury, the will to succeed. It sounds a bit picturesque, but could we inspire our new colleagues to have the courage to challenge their competitors more successfully?'

Both Pillsbury and Burger King were completely shell-shocked, short-term driven, focusing on the next quarter's results:

> I went across to Minneapolis a few days after our takeover. All the top management had bowed out by golden parachute, so we were left with a middle management, which we hoped would prove capable of running Pillsbury. We sat down with a whole bunch of them, probably 20 of us, about eight from GrandMet, which included some Americans as well as Brits, and 12 Pillsbury guys from the level below the board. We had the usual kind of GrandMet challenge debate over dinner – what made us think we could turn this business round? We worked desperately hard to get our new colleagues to join in that debate. Ian Martin [boss of GrandMet in North America] asked me what was the one thing I wanted this management to learn, and I said, 'How to fail; how to take sensible commercial risks, because if you never fail you never succeed.' Within six months Ian Martin and his team had turned them round. The amazing thing about that was that we put about ten people into Burger King from elsewhere in GrandMet, not all Brits, and probably no more than that in Pillsbury. They were very big companies but within six months one had got the businesses turned round.

While GrandMet was moving away from hotels, Ron Dennis – in a move that shocked the Formula One world – was moving away from the partnership McLaren and the cigarette company Marlboro had had for 23 years. With neither wanting to move from their negotiating position, they dissolved the partnership in 1996, and with it an image described as one of the most powerful and consistent in the sport. With it went a loss of sponsorship worth more than £30 million a year.

Dennis says it was a decision more difficult on personal than commercial grounds:

> We had had it for 23 years and for 15 of those years we had built up a tremendously close relationship with all the operating officers and all the people involved in the company on a worldwide basis. Someone would say, 'Can you do this, or can you do this in this?' Virtually anywhere in the world I could pick up the phone and make it happen, with that tremendous infrastructure and networking, to turn back on that and go back to square one, a clean piece of paper, and build up a different sort of infrastructure – which of course we have with Mercedes

Benz and all these other companies that support us – was a very hard decision. There were some personal relationships there that were very hard to break. It wasn't done for money.

The deciding point was when I looked at the line of cars in our reception area. The furthest car was made in 1980 and the closest 1995. They all looked the same because they're all painted the same, even though they're completely different, because of the design changes. We'd lost our identity. We had willingly sold our soul, almost, to Philip Morris. We were very grateful for the funds that we received and the abilities that that gave us to win the Grands Prix and finance the championships and so on. But there comes a point in your life where you have this opportunity of changing that direction and I'd had an idea for a long time, a completely different philosophy of how to market the surface of the car.

I was in an extremely difficult deadlocked situation with Philip Morris, where they weren't moving from their negotiating position and I wasn't moving from mine. To avoid an acrimonious break, we decided to have a cooling-off period in the discussions. But I was firmly convinced that the race car was wrong and they were firmly convinced it was wrong, but the other way.

Dennis was prepared to lose millions to make the change:

Even without sponsorship, the income derived from our investors was significant and I felt we'd stand a reduction in budget if it saw us pioneer that direction. We developed a strategy over the months. A month on and we started to negotiate with some companies. A lot of people come to us and we had turned them away, so it was a case of going back and saying, 'You remember, you phoned earlier.' Of course, you've got to be more disciplined and make sure you record all these things.

Out of the blue came a company, a privately owned tobacco company with a seven billion turnover. They impressed me. I started to talk to them and explain what my vision was for the future of motor sport, the branding on everything. The end result was that they agreed, which was quite radical because the simple fact is that our racing cars will look as we decide them to look. We are rebranding ourselves. What you'll be looking at is a McLaren brand and what you will see, whatever's written on the car, is McLaren's identity, not the identity of the people who invest in us. It's a quantum leap. I think that the consumer, especially the modern consumer – and I have a definition of the modern consumer – does not want a brand thrust in their face. It's a more subtle sell now, and I think that there should be more purity to the process of selling. I'm either awfully right or awfully wrong.

When Barry Hearn, rolling in snooker prize money (his players were earning 80 per cent of the total prize money in the world) decided in 1987 to move into boxing, his accountant greeted him in the mornings and asked him on an almost daily basis if he wouldn't change his mind:

> Now I want to be in boxing but there's nowhere to go, so I had to go and learn the business and I'd say it cost me between two and three million to learn the business at a time when my chief accountant would say in the morning, 'Are you absolutely sure about this?' I stayed the course and I learned the business, but it was a price to pay. Just the same as doing articles, I learnt the boxing business. Now I'm a good operator. In fact, I'm blinding.

To float, or not to float: that, on the other hand, may be the question. Some people take to the public arena like the proverbial duck in water. David Lloyd, although losing too much authority – when he sold out to Whitbread, he stayed on as a consultant then left after 14 months of reported spats – found he could only stand so far back. Others (Anita Roddick) find the culture hard to cope with.

This is what Lloyd said on the appeal of the public company before he sold out to Whitbread for £20 million:

> It hasn't changed. I value the shareholders' money as my own and I won't make any decision that's a personal decision – it's a decision for the shareholder. I'm very lucky in that I have three very strong non-executive directors and I think the non-executive position in a company is absolutely important. I phone them at least once a week. Not having gone to business school, you do need people with a different background. I've got Peter Goldstein – started Superdrug from a trolley selling in a park and turned it into a multi-million pound business, and sold out to Kingfisher. He's terrific on all the cash systems. John Hunt used to be chairman of SmithKline Beecham's product division – great on marketing and ideas, and John Rogers, who really is a professional director, knows all about the yellow book and gold book and white book and all that sort of stuff, so he's keeping us on track.

Greg Dyke made changes at London Weekend Television without compunction, slashing the staff from 1,600 to 650. He illustrates that when managing demands it, deeds will be done. Did he feel bad about 950 people losing their jobs? Not then, but now, possibly. The weight of his bad feeling, however, is directed towards the Conservative government which, he maintains, was out to tackle the TV industry because it disliked being questioned:

> We gave very high redundancy payments. Most of them were volunteers – of the 1,000, 800 to 900 volunteered. If you offered people £70,000, which is what we did for a lot of the time, and the opportunity to change their lives, a lot of people would do it. Our argument was that the business was changing and had to be restructured. It wasn't their fault. It was pretty tough, and when you look back sometimes... I didn't have any problems at the time because you don't in management. Later you look back and say was it justified, did we need to get rid of so many?
>
> There is no doubt that the Thatcherites, people I don't have a lot of time for, were after the television business and the people in it for a combination of reasons, one of them political. That lot didn't like people questioning what they did. The interesting thing is that ten years on, you can see that they were really after the BBC. ITV got savaged and the BBC survived – it's just luck, part of history. Thatcher went at a particular time. The [ITV] auction was so obviously ludicrous, and obviously ludicrous very early on. They were ridiculed for it. Finally they got a majority of 20 – you couldn't get a restructuring of the BBC through the House of Commons with a majority of 20; not a chance.

Sir Terence Conran – still making waves with his plans and projects – found that life in a public company was an enormous pleasure until things went wrong. In the end, running Storehouse in the teeth of a series of take-over bids was a trial. It was a change too far, and he walked away:

> You are responsible to a much wider band of shareholders than employees, so that was a really substantial change. One had to think about it and change one's responsibilities. I quite enjoyed it at the time. One always enjoys being chairman of a public company when it is doing well and all the analysts are saying what a hero you are. It's when you're doing badly that you start to hate it all!

12 SOMETHING VENTURED, SOMETHING LOST

The costs of success

I blank out media attention, effortlessly. I don't hear it, I don't see it. It goes with the job and if you want the job you've got to put up with what's going on and keep your focus on the way forward – the big picture.

Jack Rowell, former England rugby coach and most successful ever coach of Bath RUFC.

There is a story about Greg Dyke which he likes to tell. It starts with a return trip from Glyndebourne, at which Dyke has been entertaining an important person from the now defunct Independent Broadcasting Authority. He and his long-term partner, Sue, are returning in a chauffeured limousine. There is a bottle of champagne on hand, and both are partaking. Dyke, who has no time for delusions or illusions of grandeur, is suddenly caught short by the irony of all this: the car, the champagne, the social circles in which he now moves. He turns to Sue: 'You know what, Sue?' he says. 'We've become the people we used to want to throw bombs at.'

Becoming successful, and usually rich as a result, invariably brings a cost. To Dyke it included the realization that his values had become altered. Still a Labour supporter and donor – rejoining the party after a period at Harvard, which convinced him of the wrong-footedness and ultimate unworkability of Thatcher-style capitalism – he nevertheless acknowledges that the social firebrand in him has become compromised.

Becoming exceptionally successful, as all our subjects have, has a broad band of perceived disadvantages: publicity, which can be hurtful; lack of anonymity, which can be inconvenient; the stress usually involved in high-profile or large-scale enterprises; the shortage of time for spouses and family. Those whose personality attracts attention – Peter de Savary – or whose arena is glamorous and covetable – Ron Dennis, Jack Rowell – also find that there is nothing quite like the public enjoyment of seeing the mighty fallen. Humiliation on a grand and spotlit scale is a frightening experience. The more so because the media now have a no-holds-barred attitude to comment.

> It is probably this element of success, the exposure to the media, that is hardest to handle. Few people are capable of developing a skin so thick that vicious comment fails to pierce it. It is not possible to separate the professional and the personal to such an extent that criticism of – say – Jack Rowell the rugby coach is shrugged off by Jack Rowell the company director, or Jack Rowell the person. An interesting fact, perhaps, when it has become a convenient device, especially in business, to divorce commercial decisions from their personal repercussions.

Rowell has felt grievously wronged by the media, to such an extent that in 1996, as manager of England, he told *Guardian* sports writer Frank Keating that he would not have taken the job if he had known he would be subjected to such 'obscene' criticism:

> When I bump into various friends, they say, 'We warned you, Jack, you should never have got involved with England. How can you stand it?' These critics inhabit a sick, sad world. What justification is there for them to try and mess my life around?

Rowell found criticism of former England football manager Graham Taylor 'incredible', and said that 'nobody should be treated like that.' Later, he developed a technique for coping with unfavourable press comment: he declined to read it. Nevertheless, when Rowell looks back on his career from a chronological distance, it will be interesting to see whether the withering contempt in which he holds the media has subsided.

Rick Parry's role is less public than Rowell's, but he too has found the spotlight uncomfortable, especially during the engineering of the Premier League: 'The media attention is something I could well do without. I never enjoyed that, never enjoyed the high profile, but it was a baggage you had to carry with the job, part of the price to pay. It was too exciting a job to let slip by.'

Peter de Savary, for many years a public figure, says the scrutiny does not stop there. It extends to families, who also find their actions subjected to more than usual interest:

> You lose a lot of privacy, obviously, and are permanently under the scrutiny of the media. My wife issued a writ. This is a normal thing, but the price you pay is that you get on the train in the morning and everybody's looking at you, all of a sudden you can see they're thinking, God, how can this businessman do this to this poor farmer, etc. The price you pay is a degree of unfairness in the way the media watch your every move, and it's very hard to have any secrets, and they're right there watching it. That's a big price you pay. If things go wrong for you it is very publicly embarrassing, and it can be embarrassing for your children and the rest of your family and friends, and they can feel uncomfortable and uneasy.

Ron Dennis occasionally stops reading newspapers and listening to commentators when he feels the 'stones, arrows and knives' are penetrating. When McLaren had a long period without success – lasting for several years after a run of extraordinary triumphs – he had to switch off and take dispassionate stock. Part of this audit was to analyse the success of his company's efforts on other fronts. Part was acknowledging that soaring achievements leave greater distances to fall and people – not just in this country, but everywhere – enjoy the spectacle of the descent:

> Personally I handle it pretty easily. First of all, I know we're going to win races in the future. I absolutely know we're going to win races. It's a question of when and how much additional effort or what other changes will have to be made. The pain when you're not winning races is, to be quite honest, just taking the stones, the arrows and the knives – and there are lots of those. If you conduct your business in front of 600 million people every two weeks and you're successful, you inevitably find yourself put on a pedestal. If you're failing, then it's the opposite. People actually like to be part of the failure, they like to rip you down. It's not only in England that they rip you off the pedestal.

Dennis knows that this is because of the scale of his success, although this makes it no less painful:

> You go through periods where you don't read anything and you don't follow what people are saying. Even when the team was not winning races, mentally I was winning because I knew that the changes had been made to the company structure which would return us to the position where we would win races.
>
> There are other values by which you can judge the success of an organization. Financially, we are hugely successful in the other, less public activities we are involved with away from our F1 and road car programmes. They are programmes the public isn't aware of, and they are certainly going to come to fruition. So you know that, even when we're not winning Grands Prix, I'm pretty confident that we will get back into a winning situation. Although when you get things wrong, you feel pretty upset, most of the time I'm positive about what I'm doing.

Peter de Savary maintains that in savouring failure, the British are guilty not only of relishing it, but of ensuring that the perpetrator continues to suffer:

> One of the unattractive characteristics of this country for a businessman is that basically we do encourage people to succeed. We encourage them to do better and better and better, but we seem to have an inbuilt desire to then knock them down when we've helped put them up there. And if they fall down and fail, we are by and large a very unforgiving business society. If you have gone through bankruptcy in this country it is very, very difficult to get up again and be really successful. There are many exceptions, but generally speaking it is difficult.
>
> The opposite is true in America. People welcome you having another go. So you got it wrong last time. Have another go and they help you. It is a much more forgiving society in business terms than in this country. There is a lot more of the pioneering spirit in America than there is here, and there's the difficulty if you are not part of the so-called establishment, if you don't have strong allies and friendships and supporters. It exists throughout the country, in the City, in the Highlands of Scotland, in Cornwall – everywhere. There is an establishment and it's powerful. If you are not wired into it then it is extremely difficult to make any decent headway. In America that doesn't really exist, there is not such a structured obvious establishment. It's just a whole lot of people all having a go, a much freer business community. I find that very attractive.

Media attention is the most common set-back of becoming successful. Following is the effect on personal lives. Much is talked and written in modern Britain about having it all but, time and time again, it is demonstrated that combining a demanding career and a fulfilled, unfractured personal life exists on paper only. Long hours militate against close involvement at home. Over-busy lives can make pleasure part of the stress. For women, the attributes which are seen as admirable in men have a habit of becoming transmuted into unappealing traits.

Ron Dennis, a dispassionate and businesslike persona in commerce, is surprisingly frank, direct and personal on the toll his brilliant career has taken on his personal life. Getting married late (at 38) and being an older father is, he says, his biggest sacrifice. He made a calculated decision to delay this part of his life, believing that it could not be run in tandem with a career that was so risky.

It was deliberate. Why 38? Because at various points of my career I'd gambled everything, and you can only do that if you think, well, if everything fails, it's me; only I am going to take it. To have a family and go into financial ruin – which would have been an understatement on some of the risks that I took, calculated risks – would have increased the pressure to an unacceptable level, because I have a conscience about those things.

So I got married late and was very lucky. We initially struggled a little to have children, but now we have three. But I'm now approaching 51 and my youngest child is four and I really don't feel comfortable about that, although I know it's not unusual. I would like to have been a younger parent than I'm going to be to my kids. They're all going to go to private schools and have a great education and will get all the support through their lives that we can give them. But I don't feel comfortable about it and that was pretty much the sacrifice I felt I had made.

Given her time again, Prue Leith says she would have had another child. She has two (one adopted) and enjoyed it so much she would have liked a third. She also feels that the demands on her time have led her to 'skim':

I sometimes feel I just skim through life, that I don't properly get into anything, that I would like to know more about all sorts of things. One of the things about very busy people is that it can be just as stressful making sure you do your aerobics class and you have quality time with the children and go and have your tennis – pleasure can become a strain if you're doing too much.

Leith has, however, jealously preserved parts of her non-working life, not least by refusing to work long hours:

I am quite boring about this. I play tennis on Thursday mornings regardless (not that I'm particularly good at tennis). And I'm quite clear that I don't work at weekends. Obviously, there was a time when I was young and running my own business when I did work at weekends, but it would have to be something amazing that would stop me going home for the weekend.

Peter de Savary feels he has worked too many hours:

I work on average 12 to 14 hours a day, usually six days a week, and when I take a holiday perhaps it's a week or ten days, and I regret that. I should have spent more time over the years perhaps taking my children on holiday, spending more time with my family, and being a bit of a playboy.

Anita Roddick is sorry that becoming so successful, and having key characteristics such as tenacity, have meant that her public persona is stripped of its femininity:

You are always measured in our society, if you are successful in business, by masculine traits. You are never rewarded for bringing feminine principles into organizations. Being pushy or indomitable or intransigent are often seen as masculine. There is a lessening of sexuality, or sensuality, in people's perception. Therefore you are not a feminine woman. I don't think you should have to take on male attributes, but I think that's what is perceived.

Greg Dyke realized with a jolt, having left London Weekend following the Granada takeover, that ten years of his life had flown past without him noticing:

I looked back at ten incredibly intensive years, being three months out of it. Three months when I actually picked my kids up from school, played football with my little boy and laughed and sat around, read the paper and was amazed how quickly the days go by. First of all, I said, 'Why on earth did I work that hard?' Second, there was a bit of regret that asks what happened to those ten years. They just went. You were so concerned about this and that... whatever happened to them? They went away. There is a price for success.

Sir Terence Conran shares this sense of regret of missing important years of family life. Thrice married (and divorced) he has five children: Sebastian, Jasper, Tom, Sophie and Ned, aged from 25 to 42:

I now see more of my children than I did when they were young. Three have children of their own and they are different parents, but life was different when we were young and there was a different attitude to family life. Mothers didn't go out to work and fathers were expected to be out at work. Because my life has always been to do with work, I did work extremely hard when I was young. But they all do things related to what I do, and I think I'm closer to them now than when I was younger.

Then there's the sheer stress of being the top dog... the responsibility... the weight of it all. Some like it but, even then, not all the time.

Peter de Savary, who has chosen the commercial roller-coaster for years, wakes up some mornings filled with dread:

I wake up sometimes at four or five o'clock in the morning. I feel very depressed. I feel very worried. I feel very insecure. I feel very nervous. I wonder why the hell I'm doing this. I desperately want to sell up, live in a small cottage and run a little bistro and I know I'll be all right. By the time tea comes at seven I'm feeling a little perkier, a little more revived and self-confident and it seems to get better as the day goes by. But it is an emotional roller-coaster. Absolutely. The adrenalin highs and the lows are quite extreme. The exhilaration you feel is quite enormous and therefore it's a very emotional thing. One has to try to stay calm. One has to try not to let other people see these emotions. Something you feel inside is very different to what people perceive.

Chris Wright found, for long periods in the music business, that he was being paid for what he enjoyed doing. But football... anyone who has taken the slightest interest in football has probably read Nick Hornby's *Fever Pitch*, and anyone who has done that will understand what Wright is saying about chairing Loftus Road plc. Not only does his heart race about the fortunes of Queens Park Rangers, but also about Wasps' rugby games. It is 'bloody hard work... a damn sight more stressful than I would ever have imagined... I don't think it's a job I will do for the rest of my life... I know managers of top football teams who take beta blockers and Valium for games, because you have to do that.'

> Some people are so suited to what they do that for them, the cost of success has been small. The exposure has suited their personalities. The stress has suited their temperament. The financial rewards have suited their material pleasures.

Take Barry Hearn. He has loved being flash. He has loved being rich. He has loved being busy. The only aspect he has not enjoyed is discovering that business pacts with high stakes never lose their power to upset him:

> My biggest mistake is always trusting people. I do not learn and it drives me mad. Every time you build someone up and they rat on you or they break a contract, it really hurts. It hurts me personally because I'm too involved and I shouldn't be, and I always swear I've got to do this better. I don't want to be too cynical, I'd rather be hurt than be so cynical as to not trust anybody, but it is a mistake.

Or David Lloyd. Before the Robert Half interview, the ground was prepared at his fitness centre in Raynes Park, London. To accompany him through the doors was to walk in the shade of a man who is successful and loves it. Mobbed? Not quite, for the girls for whom Lloyd is so appealing are women, and not quite that type. But flirted with, certainly, for in the expensive cars he loves, and his understated Armani clothes, he cuts a glamorous figure who clearly enjoys this aspect of his achievement. He likes the adulation. For him, the disadvantages have been more indirect, through his family:

I don't think [success has changed me], as a person. Obviously, I don't have the mortgage on the house any more so I'm not too worried about that. I've always loved fast cars and I've always spent the maximum I could afford on a car all the way down the line

His brother, John, and ex-sister-in-law, Chris Evert, found the attention more concentrated.

When John was married to Chris they kept saying, 'These bloody reporters keep hounding me.' If you're in that business you actually want to be recognized because that's part and parcel of it. You're an entertainer, and there's nothing worse than not being recognized. I enjoy talking to people about success and I enjoy being recognized. Not, I hope, in a big-headed way, but just to talk about what we've done. If you don't want to talk about it and you aren't proud of it, what are you doing it for?

Lord Sheppard has also sloughed off the criticism of his business strategies and accepted his reputation as a tough boss. He admits to unfulfilled ambitions, but not to indulging thoughts of what might have been. The breakdown of his first marriage, he says, was not helped by his being a workaholic, despite the fact that both his wives have been unbelievably understanding. 'I've been fortunate from the point of view of having people who understood what I wanted to do. Some people would say "Bloody hell, you work night and day and think work night and day.' But if you actually enjoy that, which I do, then it's probably hard for everybody round you, but not for yourself.'

Sheppard once said the one thing he feared most was thinking, on his deathbed, 'I wish I had...' He wanted to go into politics but didn't. But he is philosophical. 'I think I would have been a diabolical backbencher. In the last few years I've got quite close to it with London First and on the board of management of the Conservative Party. But there are a million things you could do in life and unfortunately maybe we've only got one opportunity.'

To fail to do everything is human. To regret it is also human. The Ferrari, the Armani, the glamour, the money... David Lloyd would have sent it all back. If only, if only, he could have been good at golf:

If I could have swapped [business success for sporting success] I actually would have been a golfer, because I would still be playing – and there is nothing, nothing, that could ever give you the same feeling as representing your country. To go on a court and hear Great Britain against your name... you can't buy that. If I were a golfer I might be winning the Masters. To represent your country at sport is a feeling you can't buy.

The Adventure Capitalists explores, through the lives of some of Britain's best-known contemporary entrepreneurs, the mechanics of success in entrepreneurism and business, from the germ of an idea to the pressure of the public eye.

Based on interviews with each entrepreneur *The Adventure Capitalists* examines their secrets — the pain, pleasure, doubts, certainties and pitfalls — and tries to distil the essential ingredients of business success. Their backgrounds vary enormously but they all have one thing in common — each wanted to succeed.

The subjects are twelve self-starting, highly individual people as diverse as deal-maker Peter de Savary, described as 'probably Britain's purest entrepreneur', and Jack Rowell, the Oxbridge-educated, top-ranking businessman who has also managed the England rugby squad. We get the views of McLaren Formula One racing team boss, Ron Dennis; the Body Shop's redoubtable Anita Roddick; Sir Terence Conran, whose eponymous style is stamped on furniture shops and on a series of well-known restaurants; Chris Wright, founder of the Chrysalis record label and buyer of Queens Park Rangers Football Club; and Rick Parry, the manager *par excellence* who engineered the Premier League and is now chief executive of Liverpool Football Club.

Along with racquet and fitness club founder David Lloyd, former Grand Metropolitan boss Lord Sheppard, cook and businesswoman Prue Leith, boxing and snooker promoter Barry Hearn, and TV executive Greg Dyke, they are the bold, buccaneering and brave of British business across their vastly different enterprises.

The book, as well as being an entertaining read, aims to offer an insight into how these people achieved their success and seeks to unearth what has motivated them.